The Lord of Love

by LeRoy
Lawson

STANDARD PUBLISHING
Cincinnati, Ohio   39940

Unless otherwise indicated, all Scripture quotations are from the *Holy Bible, New International Version,* copyright © 1973, 1978 by the International Bible Society. Used by permission of Zondervan Bible Publishers and the International Bible Society.

Library of Congress Cataloging in Publication Data

Lawson, E. LeRoy, 1938-
  The Lord of Love.

  Includes bibliographical references.
  1. Love—Biblical teaching. 2. Bible. N.T. John—Criticism, interpretation, etc.
3. Jesus Christ—Teachings. I. Title.
BS2417.L7L39 1986   241'.4   85-9813
ISBN 0-87239-988-5
ISBN 0-87239-987-7 (instructor's ed.)

INTRODUCTION

In his play *No Exit,* Jean-Paul Sartre defines Hell as other people.

In the New Testament, God gives us a vision of Heaven. It's other people.

Since in the present or in the afterlife, we are destined to be surrounded by people, we can choose to enjoy them (and thus have a taste of Heaven) or deplore them (and fashion a Hell of our own desires). We can't escape them; we have to deal with them. It's up to us to decide what our attitude toward them will be.

The Bible speaks of an actual Heaven and an actual Hell and a divine judgment that dispatches us to one or the other. What surprises many new students of God's Word is the discovery that God does not so much judge us as allow us the consequences of our own choices. His standard of judgment has nothing to do with our strained efforts to get into Paradise. God even seems quite unimpressed by our devotion to the customary trappings of established religions. He's looking for something else.

The deciding factor, surprisingly enough, will be what we have done about love. Jesus summarizes all the law and prophets into two inseparable commandments: "'Love the Lord your God with all your heart and with all your soul and with all your mind.' This is the first and greatest commandment. And the second is like it: 'Love your neighbor as yourself.' All the Law and the Prophets hang on these two commandments'" (Matthew 22:37-40).

When Jesus speaks of the final judgment, as He does, for example, in the Parable of the Sheep and the Goats (Matthew 25:31-46), He teaches that our eternal destiny depends upon the love we have expressed for the hungry and sick and otherwise needy around us right now. As far as He is concerned, eternity has already begun for us. We are learning now the techniques for relating to other people to prepare us for an eternity with them. If we are loving the people who surround us now, we'll love being surrounded by God's people in Heaven. If we withdraw from and ignore our contemporaries, we would be miserable in the crowd around God's majestic throne in glory; they're not our kind of folks. So God will allow us to get what's coming to us, the destination for which we have so diligently prepared.

Since God's governing principle is love, then it is essential that we who have been made His children should master the art of loving. To master the subject, we must study the Master, the Lord of Love.

That's the purpose of this little book. My hope is that the readers of these pages will learn more fully how to enjoy relationships with other people. The God who ties our love of neighbor so tightly to our love of Him wants nothing so much as that you and I should express the same affection for one another that He through His Son has expressed to us. This is the secret of Heaven, that love that was born in the heart of God can be reborn in any heart that loves with the love of the Lord; it can be experienced in any church that practices what the Lord preaches; it can be broadcast into the world that God so loved that He has sent His Son to save everybody in it.

A scientist who has been doing extensive research on the human brain recently did a series of interviews on active elderly people. She found that all of these people (eighty-eight years or older) were interested in their professions even after retirement, they kept healthy bodies, and they ate an egg and drank a glass of milk each day. "And other denominators were activity, and love of life and love of others and being loved. Love is very basic."[1]

For long life, this scientist has found, "love is very basic." In our journey through John, we shall also find that for abundant life and for eternal life, love is just as basic.

May I offer a few suggestions now to you as a teacher of such an essential study? This is a very easy book for your students to read and understand. I've told lots of stories in my attempt to relate Jesus' teaching to everyday life. You shouldn't have to work very hard to explain what the Scriptural passages mean or what the author has said about those texts. If you will follow these simple steps as you prepare each lesson, you should have no difficulty in leading your class:

1) Begin your study with a period of prayer.
2) Read the Biblical text in two or three translations.

---

[1] "PT Conversation: Marian Diamond—A Love Affair with the Brain," *Psychology Today,* November 1984, p. 70.

3) Read the chapter in this book. You'll probably find it helpful to go over it at least twice, the first time fairly quickly so that you can grasp the complete treatment of the subject, the second time more slowly, marking those passages that you would like to discuss or to point out to your students.

4) Check a Bible dictionary or commentary for the meaning of any difficult words or concepts that I have failed to explain sufficiently in the chapter.

5) Look over the outline and questions in this teacher's guide.

6) Add any other questions, illustrations, or insights that will help you communicate the lesson to your students. Don't feel bound by my questions. They are designed to be discussion starters only. Most of the chapters will be provocative enough that your class members will have questions of their own.

7) Then, when you teach, be certain that you arrive early to arrange chairs for discussion, make certain that the room temperature is comfortable, greet all the class members as they enter the room (and introduce them to others, if they are new), and create an atmosphere of easy congeniality and expectation.

These are pretty traditional ideas for leading a discussion group. *The Lord of Love* requires a little extra preparation, however. You'll quickly discover as you make your way through these chapters that you can't treat the subject matter as objectively as you might like. To talk of love is to speak as a lover. Every word of the Lord on this topic pierces to the center of our being, forcing us to examine our own love life. For this, you need to arm yourself.

May I suggest you take this brief spiritual inventory before you begin teaching? It will prepare you for some of the questions you and your class will be dealing with.

1. Do I love me? Do I have a good self-image? Have I allowed the Lord who loves me to help me learn to accept and love myself? Will I project a healthy self-respect to my students? Have I kept my self-love in check, so that it hasn't been warped into a sickly pride or egotism?

2. Do I love my family? It's at home that we learn how to "give and take." Have I come from a loving home—and have I returned my parents' love? Do I live in one? If married, does my spouse receive constant reminders of my love? If a parent, do my children feel secure in my unqualified love for them? If single, have I dealt with any incipient feelings of rejection or bitterness? Have I reached out to others who form my "adopted" family?

3. Do I love the Lord? The Bible says that I am to have no other god before God. Do I put God first? Before everyone and everything else? Do I love Him for my sake? Or His sake? Or both? How do I express my love of the Lord? How can I show someone who doesn't know God just how much I love Him?

4. Do I love the ones my Lord loves? "God so loved the world...." Do I love His world? Christ commissioned His disciples to go into all the world to make disciples. Does He include me in that commission? What exactly does love demand? What contribution to God's work on earth am I making through my church?

5. Do I love my class? Why am I teaching? Whom am I teaching? Do I love my students enough to get to know them personally? To spend extra time with them individually? To prepare to give my very best for them? To genuinely care about helping them to become better acquainted with my Lord?

The inventory could be more extensive, but these questions should be sufficient to help you—as they have helped me—to be impressed with the scope of these demanding lessons. Love demands our best, our all.

The Lord of Love is based on the life and teachings of Jesus in the Gospel of John. You may be disappointed, even as I am, that some familiar passages in the Gospel are not studied, but the limitations of time and space prevented a more exhaustive study. You will find, though, that there is enough here to keep a class struggling to explore the many implications of the meaning of love that these thirteen chapters introduce. I hope you and your students will fill in the gaps through your devotional study of the entire Gospel.

COURSE PLAN

The Lord of Love was written specifically as the adult lesson material for the Vacation Bible School series of the same name. I also have had Sunday-morning adult Bible classes in mind, as well as evening Bible-study groups. Of course, the book can also serve as a guide for personal devotional study of the Gospel of John or an individual exploration of the many implications of love.

vi

If you are using the book for Vacation Bible School, the editors suggest that for the five-session study you select chapters 1, 3, 5, 7, and 9.

If you have ten sessions, the editors recommend that you study chapters 1-9 and chapter 13.

My hope, of course, is that no matter how many class periods you have, you will read the entire book so that you will approach each chapter with a knowledge of the whole.

LESSON PLANS

I. LIKE FATHER, LIKE SON

Text: John 1:1-18; 1 John 4:8
Theme: The love of Jesus is the love of God.
Outline:
 I. What is God like?
   He is like Jesus.
II. What is love like?
   Love is like Jesus.

Discussion Questions:
   1. *Is* God always loving?
   2. Does God will everything that happens?
   3. What is the best way to learn about the nature of God?
   4. When we use the word *God,* are we telling more about God or about ourselves?
   5. How would you define love?
   6. How does our society define it?
   7. How does the Bible define it?
   8. Describe the love of God as if you were talking to a preschool child; then to a teenager; then to a college student; finally to a grandfather. Is there any difference from one description to the next?
   9. How does one "give of himself" to another?
   10. In John 1:29-34, Jesus is called the "Lamb of God." Why does John the Baptist use this title for Him? What does it teach about love?

II. POWER *FOR* THE PEOPLE

Text: John 2:1-16
Theme: Love and Power
Outline: In two celebrations, Jesus unleashes His power on behalf of people.
  I. Celebration of Life
 II. Celebration of God

Discussion Questions:

1. What do these two incidents (the wedding feast and the cleansing of the temple) have in common? What do they tell us about Jesus?

2. What does the wedding feast tell us about Jesus' "love of life"? Is there a place for such celebration, then, in *our* lives?

3. What does the wedding feast incident tell us about the purpose of religion?

4. Why did Jesus' contemporaries enjoy "hanging around with Him"?

5. Should we laugh in church?

6. What should we conclude about the place of anger? Is it ever justified? Is there such a thing as "righteous indignation"? Is anger safe?

7. How is it possible to channel anger?

8. What makes God angry?

9. What is the relationship of love to power?

III. THE LORD LOVES YOU AS YOU ARE

Text: John 3:16, 17; 4:1-29
Theme: Love and Acceptance
Outline:
  I. The Lord of Love gives acceptance
 II. The Lord of Love gives forgiveness
III. The Lord of Love gives us a lift

Discussion Questions:

1. Three types of prejudice are discussed here: racial and religious, social, and sexist. Is any one of these a problem in your town?

2. What kinds of risks was Jesus running in speaking to the Samaritan woman?

3. This chapter says that love must begin with acceptance. What does this mean? Why is it so? Or is it?

4. Is it possible for a person to function without prejudices?

5. How did Jesus show that He had accepted the Samaritan woman? How do we exhibit acceptance?

6. What makes listening so hard?

7. Why is it so difficult for us to accept the fact that God accepts us?

8. Does acceptance always imply forgiveness, as this chapter says?

9. Do you think that there is such a thing as "God-hunger"? Who is afflicted with it?

10. How does Jesus "give us a lift"?

IV. TAKING THE LORD OF LOVE AT HIS WORD

Text: John 4:46-54; 14:23; 15:9-17
Theme: Love and obedience
Outline:
  I. He "took Jesus at his word ..."
 II. "He will obey my teaching"
III. "If you obey ... you will remain in my love"
  A. "That your joy may be complete"
  B. "Greater love ... that one lay down his life for his friends"
  C. "You are my friends if you do what I command"

Discussion Questions

1. Under the circumstances of John 4:46-54, would you have obeyed Jesus?

2. Does this make sense? "Love demands obedience; obedience leads to greater love."

3. What do you think of Macdonald's statement? "Oh, the folly of any mind that would explain God before obeying Him!"

4. What does this mean: "A mind believes, but it takes a whole person to love."

5. Is there danger in obedience? If so, how can it be avoided?

6. What does it mean for us to be "friends" of Jesus?

ix

7. What is the best way for us to show how much we love the Lord?

8. "Saving lives is all a part of our day's work." Do you agree? How do we do this work?

9. Is there anything more that we should be doing to prove we take the Lord of Love at His word?

V. LOVE ISN'T EITHER BLIND!

Text: John 9:1-39
Theme: Love and Seeing Clearly

Discussion Questions:

1. Christians love to tell what the Lord has done for them. Take a little time to share your testimonies with each other.

2. What is the relationship of love and faith? How does really loving someone help us to see more clearly?

3. Why did the Pharisees have so much trouble accepting the fact that Jesus had healed the blind man? What kept them from seeing? (Any lesson for us here?)

4. If one's religious faith is genuine, this chapter teaches, it is in the conscience that he first feels its impact. Is this true? How has your faith changed your conscience?

5. This chapter tells several conversion stories. Note how conversion leads to a change of behavior. Is it possible to be converted and not change?

6. Why couldn't John Quincy Adams change his personality?

7. In this Scripture, Jesus states His reason for coming into the world. What is it?

8. In what ways would our nation change if we really became convicted that the way of the Lord of Love is superior?

VI. LOVE GIVES IT ALL

Text: John 10:1-18
Theme: Love and Sacrifice
Outline:
 I. To love is to do
 II. To love is to pay the price

Discussion Questions:

1. Why would a man allow himself to drown in order to save five strangers?
2. Are there hirelings among religious leaders today? How can you recognize them? How, then, can you distinguish a true shepherd?
3. What makes love so difficult to achieve?
4. Is the love of a *kamikaze* pilot for his country the same kind of love Jesus wants of His disciples for one another?
5. How did Mrs. Tolstoy express her love for her husband? How does today's wife? Or today's husband?
6. Philip Caputo was ready to lay down his life for a ribbon. What would you be willing to sacrifice everything for?
7. What is the mark of a good teacher? Of a good parent? Of a good pastor? Of a good president?
8. Is Dr. Claude Barlow a good example of sacrificial love?
9. Is this true? "There is no love without sacrifice."

VII. THE LORD OF LOVE IS PRO-LIFE

Text: John 11:25
Theme: Love and the Sanctity of Life
Outline:
  I. In the beginning of life
 II. At the end, also
III. And in the living of your days

Discussion Questions:

1. What does "pro-life" mean?
2. How shall we define life? Flesh and blood? Body and soul?
3. What does Psalm 139:13-16 tell us about God's appreciation of an unborn baby?
4. Is what we do with our bodies any business of God's?
5. What assurance do we have of life after death?
6. What does the Bible teach us about the nature of our resurrection body? (See 1 Corinthians 15.)
7. What do Jesus' words mean to you? "I am the resurrection *and* the life."
8. If you could do whatever you felt you needed to do in order to make your life perfect now, what would you change?

9. Discuss how your acceptance of Christ as Lord has made your life more abundant now.

VIII. LOVE WASHES DIRTY FEET

Text: John 13:1-17
Theme: Love and Humility
Outline:
  I. Humility expresses love
 II. Humility assumes confidence—in self and in God
III. Humility receives its own reward

Discussion Questions:
  1. Discuss how the rulers of the Gentiles "lord it over" them. Are we guilty of the same?
  2. What makes us so conscious of titles, uniforms, and status symbols?
  3. Does Jesus really expect us to act like servants? Won't people take unfair advantage of us? Won't they despise, rather than love, us?
  4. Is this true? "Without humility, there is no love."
  5. Why do you think the towel and washbasin have never been accepted as popular Christian symbols?
  6. In what way is self-love related to humility?
  7. What is the true source of a Christian's self-confidence?
  8. Why must humility be present before there can be any genuine fellowship between people?
  9. What are the rewards of humility you seek the most?
10. A minister once pointed out that there is a parallel between science and society: Men master natural law by scientific humility and master other men by humble service. Do you agree?

IX. TO BE OR NOT TO BE

Text: John 12:20-33
Theme: Love and death
Outline:
  I. To succeed, you must be prepared to lose

II. To live, you must be prepared to die
III. To love, you must hate
IV. To serve the Lord, you must follow Him

Discussion Questions:

1. Jesus transforms His death into something glorious. Have you known other persons who served the Lord as effectively in dying as they did in living?

2. Have you ever been in the position of either Gary Bettenhausen or Benjamin Franklin? How did you decide what was the right thing to do? In other words, what is the basis of your system of values?

3. *Is* discretion always the better part of valor?

4. What do you think of Dr. William L. Mellon's decision to become a doctor—in Haiti?

5. "Love doesn't bloom unless first there is a death," this chapter says. What kind of death?

6. Jesus said, "It was for this reason I came to this hour." How does your love help you discover the reason for which you are now living—or dying?

7. Were you taught that Christians must never hate? How then do you handle this passage?

8. How would Jesus have us follow Him? What is to become our cross?

9. What is the source of our security?

X. UNAFRAID OF TOMORROW

Text: John 14:1-7
Theme: Love and Trust
Outline:
 I. You can believe in me—I would not lie to you
 II. You can trust me—I want you to be with me forever
III. You can walk with me—I will lead you
IV. You can face your future with hope

Discussion questions:

1. Why are so many people afraid of the future?

2. Where do you turn when it seems that everything in your life is falling apart?

3. "Become more personal with your faith," this chapter says, but how can we do that?

4. Why should we believe that Jesus is telling the truth?

5. What are some of your favorite Scriptures relating to this subject of love and trust? Which ones do you meditate on when you are troubled?

6. Have you ever been lost? What got you out? Are you more comforted by a map or a guide?

7. In your own words, what does this verse mean to you? "I am the way, and the truth, and the life."

8. What is there to be afraid of in the Christian message?

XI. HOW TO HANDLE REJECTION

Text: John 15:18-27
Theme: Love and Rejection
Outline:
 I. Remember your Lord
 II. Remember: You made your choice
III. Let the Lord help you
IV. Keep on loving

Discussion Questions:

1. Have you ever experienced rejection of your love? Perhaps you would be willing to share how you handled it so that what you learned can be of help to others.

2. The world hated Jesus because of His teaching and in spite of His great works. Can you give some examples of the abuse Jesus suffered in spite of His love?

3. There is a lot of "getting even" in life, isn't there? Why won't Jesus let us go along with everybody else?

4. "You can't belong to Christ and at the same time be fully acceptable to the world that wants nothing to do with Him or His." What, then, should we expect as Christians?

5. What is the Holy Spirit's role in our attempt to handle rejection?

6. How does the Bible help us?

7. "Love them—for their sake, for your sake, for God's sake." How does love benefit each?

8. What do you do when you are knocked down in life?

9. Machiavelli says in *The Prince* that "hatred is acquired as much by good works as by bad ones." Is it worth it, then, to devote so much energy to doing good?

10. Dryden wrote in the eighteenth century,

> Pains of love be sweeter far
> Than all other pleasures are.

Can you agree with him, or does he seem a little idealistic? What is one of the pains of rejection?

XII. LOVE REACHES OUT AND HANGS ON

Text: John 17:20-26
Theme: Love and Sharing the Gospel (evangelism and Christian unity)
Outline:
 I. Love reaches out
II. Love hangs on

Discussion Questions:
1. What has kept Christianity from sweeping the world's population into its embrace?

2. How did Jesus expect the world to be evangelized?

3. What does evangelism have to do with love?

4. What do you think of E. Stanley Jones' definition of the church as "a society of organized love"? Does your church function this way?

5. Have you asked, "For whom am I crying? Whose wounds am I binding? Is my love reaching out?"

6. Is it possible to "sneak into Heaven incognito"?

7. Do you agree that "the church exists primarily for the sake of those who don't yet belong to it"? How, then, does your church reach out to them?

8. What is the difference between unity and uniformity? Which does Jesus pray for?

9. Is unity among Christians possible? What will we have to do to achieve it?

10. What two bases does Christian unity have, according to this chapter? Do you agree with the author? If so, why? If not, what do *you* think is the basis of unity?

XIII. WHAT DOES GOD WANT ME TO DO WITH MY LIFE?

Text: John 21:15-19
Theme: Love and Renewal
Outline:
  I. Call
 II. Apprenticeship
III. Crisis
IV. Reassurance
 V. Renewal

Discussion Questions:
1. Where do you go to find out about your future?
2. What advice would you give a young college woman who seeks to know what to do with the rest of her life? What do you think of the advice in this chapter?
3. The first step in doing what God wants is to obey His invitation to follow Jesus. Why Jesus? Why not some other great religious leader, like Moses or David or Mohammed or Billy Graham?
4. What is an apprentice? Would you consider yourself an apprentice of Jesus? What does it mean to be a "disciple" of Jesus?
5. What are we trying to learn from Jesus?
6. Why did Peter fail his big test? What caused him to desert Jesus? Could it happen to us?
7. How did Jesus reassure Peter that, even though the disciple deserted the Master, the Master still wanted Peter to be His friend?
8. Why did Jesus ask Peter three times about the depth of his love?
9. What did Jesus require of Peter as proof of that love?
10. What does He require of us? Isn't this the same as asking, "What does God want me to do with my life?" Isn't God always concerned about His sheep?
11. The question for each of us, then, is this: "What am I doing right now to take care of God's sheep?" What is your answer?

The
Lord
of
Love

by LeRoy
Lawson

STANDARD PUBLISHING
Cincinnati, Ohio   39941

Unless otherwise indicated, all Scripture quotations are from the *Holy Bible, New International Version,* copyright © 1973, 1978 by the International Bible Society. Used by permission of Zondervan Bible Publishers and the International Bible Society.

Expressing the views of his own heart, the author may express views not entirely consistent with those of the publisher.

Library of Congress Cataloging in Publication Data

Lawson, E. LeRoy, 1938-
  The Lord of Love.

  Includes bibliographical references.
  1. Love—Biblical teaching. 2. Bible. N.T. John—Criticism, interpretation, etc. 3. Jesus Christ—Teachings. I. Title.
BS2417.L7L39   1986   241′.4   85-9813
ISBN 0-87239-988-5
ISBN 0-87239-987-7 (instructor's ed.)

CONTENTS

INTRODUCTION

I wish I had been there when Eric Duggins was ordained as a foreign missionary. I had been his minister in his younger years and had been proud of his growing conviction that God wanted him to serve Him abroad. Eric had moved on for further education, and I had accepted the call to serve in another city, so I missed this important occasion.

Had I been able to participate, there are many things I would have wished to say to him. Ever since my ordination a quarter of a century ago, I have never failed to be humbly awed by the significance of this dedication of a life to full-time Christian ministry. You can count on it, I would have done my best to find the right words to challenge Eric to give of his best for the Master.

My presence wasn't missed, however. Keith Shafer, one of the church's finest elders, delivered a charge that said everything I could have offered for the occasion. He called on Eric to serve the Lord of Love with the love of the Lord:

> I want to remind you that the road will not always be easy. The ambassador for Christ should not only minister to men in the spirit of joyful service, but he should gladly spend and be spent for them, even though his service be met with indifference, ingratitude, and hate. Like his Lord, he should have a love for men so great that it will outlive misunderstanding, misrepresentation, insult, and injury, and go on revealing itself day after day in a self-sacrificing labor. *Develop a love that forgives the coldest indifference, the deepest ingratitude, the bitterest hate, the cruelest wrong, and gives back in fullest measure good for the evil.*

Mr. Shafer knows something of the demands of love, doesn't he? His challenge may have been specifically written for Eric, but it applies to every believer in Christ. As we believe, so we love.

Keith Shafer's description recalls the incomparable words of the Apostle Paul in 1 Corinthians:

> This love of which I speak is slow to lose patience—it looks for a way to be constructive; it is not possessive: it is neither anxious to impress nor does it cherish inflated ideas of its own importance.

5

Love has good manners and does not pursue selfish advantage. It is not touchy. It does not keep account of evil or gloat over the wickedness of other people.

On the contrary, it shares the joy of those who live by the truth. Love knows no limit to its endurance, no end to its trust, no fading of its hope; it can outlast anything. Love never fails (1 Corinthians 13:4-8, J. B. Phillips translation).

It's tough love, isn't it? The Biblical word for it is *agape,* the highest of Christian virtues. *Agape* is the term for the love of God. Remarkably, the very same word refers as well to human love. That it can be employed to speak of the love of both God and man indicates that the Bible doesn't draw our usual strict distinction between them. To the contrary, the Bible urges humanity to love with the love of God. It does even more: it details exactly what God's love is like. It's like Jesus.

In the life of Jesus, divine love is expressed through a Person. As Son of God, He brings love to earth; as Son of Man, He lives human life at its highest, loveliest level. In Christ, we learn what a difference love makes in our lives!

Several years ago, I read Viktor Frankl's helpful little book *Man's Search for Meaning.* In it, the famed psychologist recounts his days in Nazi concentration camps. Describing inhuman treatment so incredible that only a term like "holocaust" can come close to hinting at the horror, Dr. Frankl recalls how in the midst of his deprivations, his mind became transfixed on the truth proclaimed by so many thinkers as "the final wisdom." This truth is "that love is the ultimate and the highest goal to which man can aspire." He calls this "the greatest secret that human poetry and human thought and belief have to impart: *The salvation of man is through love and in love.*" [1]

If Frankl and his fellow thinkers on the subject of "the final wisdom" are correct, then we must take love very seriously. We Christians go one step beyond Frankl, though. We understand that salvation is not through some concept called love, nor through our fallible human efforts to try to love, but through the One who revealed and embodied love. He lived love and He died for love so that He can forever offer us life in the power of His love.

---

[1] Victor Frankl, *Man's Search for Meaning* (New York: Washington Square Press, 1963), pp. 57-59

This little study book is my attempt to offer some insights into the Biblical meaning of love. It focuses on the ministry of Jesus because He is the Lord of Love.

Our principle text is the Gospel of John. We are severely limiting ourselves because of the strictures of space and time. Otherwise, we could enjoyably pursue the theme throughout the entire New Testament—and dip into the Old for additional insight.

For now, though, we'll confine ourselves to John—and in John, to just a few passages. I hope that I have included enough, however, to whet your appetite for more study.

A word of caution. Be prepared to put your study into service. Jesus won't let His disciples confine themselves to a study *about* love. He expects—in fact, He commands—us to do more: to serve Him and one another *in* love.

We must obey His command. He is the *Lord* of love.

1

LIKE FATHER, LIKE SON

John 1:1-18

A book about the Lord of Love must start with that simple text every Sunday-school child learns: "God is love" (1 John 4:8). No verse is easier for a little boy or girl to memorize nor harder for an adult to fully appreciate. The words come quickly to the tongue, but for most of us, the meaning takes a lifetime to comprehend. It speaks of God and love, but just who is God, anyway, and what is meant by love?

What Is God Like?

We begin with the first part of the verse, changing the question just a bit. The Bible never tells us exactly who God is, since our finite human vocabulary lacks the precise words to define Him. Instead, as we shall see in this chapter, the Scriptures give us several hints about His nature, and by putting all of them together, we can come close to a workable understanding of Him. When the Sunday-school pupil recites, "God is love," he isn't telling everything there is to say about God; he is just pointing out what is most important about Him.

You may already be tempted to put this book down, especially if your experience has taught you to think of God as almost anything but loving. A close friend of mine has wrestled for years with the question of the nature of God. Her Sunday-school teachers taught her that God is love, but her traumatic childhood made her want to run away from Him. Her strict, unfair, neurotic parents often inflicted severe punishments on her, and they invoked God's wrath as they whaled away.

I am thinking also of a middle-aged man who sought relief in counseling. His psychologist employed hypnosis to help him return to his childhood to get at the root of his difficulties, which turned out to be the death of his father. As he relived the terrible event, the man screamed, "I hate you, God. I hate you. You killed my daddy."

In the conversation following the outburst, the wise Christian

9

counselor did not argue with the man or preach that it was wrong to hate God. Instead, he assured him that the boy he used to be had every reason to hate a god who kills little boys' daddies. What he needed to understand now, however, was that the god the little boy had learned to despise so many years ago was not the true God. He then described the God of love.

For years, I have listened as confused or angry men and women described this or that frightening event in their lives—the death of a parent, the lingering illness of a loved one, a national or international tragedy—and then announced, "I can't believe in a God who would do a thing like that!"

I have certainly sympathized with their emotion, but I have also had to explain that they have made a dangerous assumption. They think that God wills everything that happens; so they hold Him responsible for the grief in their lives. They are like the little boy whose father died. Since he believed there was a God, and he had been taught that God is all-powerful, he reasoned that this all-powerful God must have killed his daddy. I can't believe in a god like that, either.

This assumption is dangerous because once we've prematurely made up our minds exactly what God is like, we aren't very open to hear what God tells us about himself. We could as easily end up hating God, and feeling guilty for our hatred, as the middle-aged man who carried in him a little boy's resentment against God for something God didn't do.

You may wonder by what right the counselor gave the man permission to yell at God for his father's death. What made him so sure that the true God doesn't "kill" daddies? How did he know? Where did he learn so much about God? How could he so confidently tell his distraught client that the god he hated was not God?

The answer to all these questions is the same: he learned about God from the same source we have, the Bible. But this is not in itself a satisfactory answer, is it? Too many people read the Bible and come to incomplete or contradictory pictures of God. For instance, one young Christian, wanting to learn something of God, decided to begin reading on the first page of Genesis and keep reading until he reached the last chapter of Revelation. When he read through the historical books of the Old Testament, however, he was astonished at the bloody wars fought in the name of God as the Israelites captured and settled their promised land.

10

He could not believe that God would allow such carnage. "What kind of God is He, anyway?" he asked.

He was not the first to be offended or confused. To read the Bible without first understanding what God is telling us about himself in Jesus is to be left with many possible, and they would be mostly wrong, ideas.

The Bible presents God in many roles. He is the Holy, Almighty, Unchanging, Infinite One who is Judge, Creator, Wisdom, Spirit, King, Jealous Lover, Owner of all that is, the All-Knowing, All-wise, All-powerful Governor of the universe. So many words are used to describe Him in Scripture and elsewhere, and from so many points of view, that His essence gets lost in our language. You can understand why some poets like Alexander Pope give up and accept just about any concept of God:

> Father of all! in ev'ry age,
> In ev'ry clime adored,
> By saint, by savage, and by sage,
> Jehovah, Jove, or Lord!

But this easy tolerance blurs any lines of distinction between the true God and all the counterfeits. If anybody's idea of God is as good as anybody else's, then no one's is worth anything. If God exists, and if He can be known at all, then we must be satisfied with nothing less than true knowledge of Him. Otherwise when we use the word *God,* we aren't saying so much about God as we are about ourselves.

This reminds us of Francis Bacon's wise words, "The world as Plato describes it is merely a world constructed by Plato, and pictures Plato rather than the world." We all tend to use religious language in the same way. Our words don't express so much about God as about ourselves.

But we really do want to learn about God, and if we can't trust the words people use to talk about Him, and we can't even be certain that we are reading the Bible correctly, is there any way to be sure of what God is like?

He Is Like Jesus

Yes, there is. We can take seriously what John says in the prologue of his Gospel. We can accept the fact that God is Christlike. This sounds so simple, doesn't it? Perhaps too simple. I had been a Christian for many years and had struggled over the nature

11

of God for most of those years before I fully realized how much more complicated I was making my Christian faith than it needed to be. I had been searching for philosophical explanations of the existence of God. Instead of reading the Gospels to learn what God has communicated about himself in Jesus, I started with jaw-breaking philosophical concepts like omniscience, omnipresence, omnipotence, trinity, the argument from cosmogony, and so on. My enlarging vocabulary sounded impressive (at least to my sophomoric ears) but all my big words didn't bring me any closer to a knowledge of God. What grief I could have saved myself if I had just turned to John 1:1-18 first. Here, in the easiest, clearest words he could find, John tells us that God is Christlike. If you really want to know God, you must know Jesus, for Jesus is all of God that our finite human minds can comprehend. We may not be able to understand everything about God, but we can know Jesus, and He's enough. Since "God was pleased to have all his fullness dwell in [Jesus]" (Colossians 1:19), to know Him is to know God.

"In the beginning was the Word, and the Word was with God, and the Word was God. He was with God in the beginning.

"Through him all things were made; without him nothing was made that has been made. . . .

"No one has ever seen God, but God the only Son, who is at the Father's side, has made him known" (John 1:1-3, 18).

John writes with the simple clarity of a wise man who has found the truth and will not be tempted by anything less. He wants us to know God, so he introduces us to Jesus, who reveals His Father to us.

Dr. James Dobson helps us grasp how the Son reveals the Father. It has happened in *his* family. The famous Christian psychologist describes his work as a family counselor as an extension of his father's ministry. The older Dobson said one day that God had revealed to him that his message was going to reach millions of people, expanding beyond every expectation.

But it didn't happen. Although the senior Dobson was considered quite a successful minister, his work never did reach such proportions in his lifetime. His son, however, is one of the best known Christian leaders in our day. His message regarding the Christian family has been spread through books, lectures, magazines, and radio and television broadcasts all around the world. Dr. Dobson says, "I see all that's happened to me having very little to do with my own talent or ability or dedication. I see it as a continuation of my father's ministry and a fulfillment of the promise God made to him over 40 years ago."[1] Everyone who has listened much to Dr. Dobson has heard many tributes to the wisdom and teaching of his father. It is obvious that the father's message has indeed reached millions through the son.

Whoever has listened to Jesus has likewise listened to His Father as well, since "the very work that the Father has given me to finish, and which I am doing, testifies that the Father has sent me" (John 5:36). The Lord insists that "the Father is in me, and I in the Father" (John 10:38) and that "whatever I say is just what the Father has told me to say" (John 12:50).

What Is Love Like?

If it is true that when we look at Jesus, we see His Father living in flesh among us, it is equally true that in the Son we see the Father's love as well. Jesus acts out God's love for us. In the prologue of his Gospel, John calls Jesus "the true light that gives light to every man (1:9)." The Light shines on God and reveals His love; the Light also shines on man and exposes our need for love—a need to receive the love of God and a need to become a channel through which God's love can flow to others.

What can we say about love that hasn't already been said many times and in many ways? Scholars never tire of reminding us that the Greeks had several words that are translated by our one word *love*, each one highlighting a characteristic of this complex concept. The Greeks adored *eros*, which is physical attraction, bodily love that loves if its love is returned. They also enjoyed *phileo*, the love of brother for brother. But the highest form in the Bible is *agape*, which is love like God's love.

Our definitions just can't do justice to *agape*. Leslie Weatherhead tries to capture it ("a sustained determination to show unbreakable good will in order that the best qualities in the person 'loved' may be called forth"[2]), but his precise language can't catch its full essence. Stephen Neill's "steady directing of the

---

[1] "Snatching the Family from Its Grave," *Christianity Today* (May 7, 1982), p. 15.

[2] *The Significance of Silence* (New York: Abingdon-Cokesbury, 1945), p. 64.

13

human will toward the eternal well-being of another"[3] doesn't do much better.

Action

The power of *agape* is in the fact that it can be commanded by our wills rather than dictated by our feelings. It is subject to our control, so we can hold on to it in spite of what happens to us. This love keeps on hanging on—it is eternal. Its opposite is not hate, as it would be if love were only a feeling, but indifference, apathy, a decision not to care anymore.

It is this deliberate, willful love that God expresses in Christ. This love is sacrificial, risk-taking goodwill. It loves even when its affection is not reciprocated. Jesus came to His own people, but they rejected Him. They murdered Him, yet He kept on loving.

I was talking the other day with a discouraged young man who is approaching the marrying age but has no prospects. He hasn't even been dating. Although he didn't want to say so, he finally admitted that his real problem is that he is afraid of women. More specifically, he is afraid of being rejected by women. He doesn't want to run the risk of being humiliated if his advances are spurned, yet he dreams of being married and raising a family.

What could I say to encourage him? I had to admit he is right. Yes, he'll be rejected. Yes, he'll be humiliated. There's no doubt he'll be hurt. Yet he must hazard the dangers of love or resign himself to bachelorhood.

He wanted to know how he could protect himself. I'm afraid I didn't have a satisfactory solution for him. I know many people who work very hard to protect themselves from being hurt. They devote themselves to their hobbies or careers or some other pursuit in order to keep themselves unentangled by any potentially hurtful relationships with people. The result is they have kept their hearts from being broken, but not from becoming hardened. They aren't vulnerable any more, but neither are they soft and warm and caring. They have erected such defenses that no one can get close to them. I couldn't recommend such a fate for my friend. I suggested instead that he learn more about the love of the Lord.

If God is our example (Ephesians 5:1), then we need to reread the Bible to find out how He loves. A surprise is in store for those

---

[3]Quoted in F. D. Coggan, *The New Testament Basis of Moral Theology* (London: Tyndale Press, 1948), p. 8.

14

who think of Him as a vengeful or bloodthirsty deity. In the Old Testament, we read of the God who takes care of widows, whose helping hand goes out to orphans, who insists on special treatment for the poor and strangers and servants. He lays down rules like the Sabbath so that even working animals can have a little rest. Trees and birds don't escape His careful attention, either. He is always "a gracious and compassionate God, slow to anger and abounding in love ..." (Jonah 4:2). God seems to be like the mother of twelve children in a treasured old story. When she was asked, "Which one of your children do you love most? she answered, "The one who is sick until he gets well. The one who is away until he comes home. The one who is in trouble until he is safe."[4]

As a caring parent, God also takes care of his rebellious, troubled, wayfaring children. The Divine Parent becomes the loving Savior in Jesus. So if we really wish to understand the love of God, we must study the life of Christ. He is the love of God in action. In Jesus, God gives himself for our sakes.

This is not a bad definition by the way: Love is self-giving. On this point, most writers agree. Erich Fromm's famous little book, *The Art of Loving,* explains it this way:

> "What does one person give to another? He gives of himself, of the most precious he has, he gives of his life. This does not necessarily mean that he sacrifices his life for the other—but that he gives him of that which is alive in him; he gives him of his joy, of his interest, of his understanding, of his knowledge, of his humor, of his sadness—of all expressions and manifestations of that which is alive in him."[5]

Fromm writes as a student of the subject, but not necessarily as a student of Jesus, who stands as the world's supreme example of love. Because of His crucifixion, we now perceive that agape love gives until there is nothing left to give—it gives itself completely, even to self-sacrifice.

Love is like Jesus, who gave His all for our sake.

---

[4]William Graham Cole, *Sex and Love in the Bible* (New York: Association Press, 1959), p. 46.

[5]*The Art of Loving.* Quoted in *Literary Reflections,* Williams R. Elkins, Jack L. Kendall, John R. Willingham, eds. (New York: McGraw-Hill Book Company, 1982), p. 214.

Love Is Like Jesus

God's love, then, is Christlike. I like the lesson a wise old monk in the Middle Ages taught his people. He announced that he would preach in the cathedral one evening on the subject of the love of God. The people assembled, standing in silence as they waited for the service to begin, the sun's light streaming through the stained-glass windows; then, when the last ray of light was gone, the monk took a burning candle from the candelabrum, walked to a life-sized statue of Christ on the cross, and held the flame near the wounds on His feet, then His hands, then His side. Still without a word, he finally held the light up to the crown of thorns on Jesus' brow.

He never spoke a word, but people wept in the silence. He had helped them appreciate the love of God.[6]

The monk wisely moved his congregation's attention from the beauty of the sun's rays penetrating the stained-glass windows to the ugly scars on Jesus' body. Here is love in action. Real love is not always beautiful nor pleasant to look upon. The beauty of God's creation can leave one moved but unmoving. God could not enjoy His handiwork in nature when the crown of His creation, man, was suffering the consequences of rebellion. His love moved Him to action; He had to do something. It would be costly, His suffering would be brutal, but He couldn't turn His back on man, even though man had rejected Him. He still loved the unlovely.

"You see, at just the right time, when we were still powerless, Christ died for the ungodly. . . . God demonstrates his own love for us in this: While we were still sinners, Christ died for us" (Romans 5:6, 8).

Not only did Jesus die for us, but He has also made it possible, John says (John 1:13), for us to become children of God!

I read recently that the average American parents to whom a son was born in 1982 can expect to spent $141,623 (in 1982 dollars) to raise him to the age of 22. This enormous financial cost is only one of the prices parents pay. There are also the worry, the emotional stress, the disappointments, and the multiplied trials that every conscientious parent undergoes for the sake of the

---

[6]J. Wallace Hamilton, *Who Goes There?* (Westwood, NJ: Fleming H. Revel Co., 1958), p. 130.

16

child. It is no wonder that several years ago, columnist Ann Landers, in a poll she conducted asking parents, "If you had it to do all over again, would you still have a family?" found that nearly fifty percent answered that they wouldn't.

Miss Landers' research has been further supported by recent studies reporting that in America some 5.2 million children are in day care in private homes, 900,000 attend licensed day-care centers, and 1.6 million are cared for by relatives. There are another 5.3 million preteenage children of working parents who seem to be cared for by no one.

It is costly to be a parent. Yet the heavenly Parent has paid the ultimate cost in order that we can be and remain His children!

If you still have any doubt about God's love for you, reread Jesus' set of three parables in Luke 15. In these little stories of a lost sheep, a lost coin, and a lost son, Jesus defends himself from the religious leaders' charge that He was eating with sinners. Jesus doesn't deny that He is guilty as charged, but offers as His defense that God loves every sinner who repents and returns to Him. He is like the grieving father who cannot rest until his rebellious son returns to his loving, forgiving, accepting arms.

You wouldn't expect less, would you, from the Lord of Love?

2

POWER *FOR* THE PEOPLE

John 2:1-16

At first, the two incidents recorded in John 2:1-16 don't seem to have anything in common. In the former one, Jesus accommodates His mother by performing a miracle to prevent embarrassment at a wedding feast. In the second one, he lashes out in anger against money changers and hucksters in the temple. The two events could hardly seem more dissimilar—until, with further thought, we detect the one thing that holds them together.

That one thing is power. In both instances, because of His love for the people involved, Jesus unleashes His miraculous authority and keeps two quite different forms of celebration alive. He first blesses a wedding celebration that has run out of its essential wine, and then He attacks exploiters who have made a mockery of people's celebration of God. In each case, Jesus demonstrates that His is power *for* the people.

Celebration of Life

Palestinian life in Jesus' day was harsh by today's standards. It was tough to scratch out a living with a scorching sun overhead, rocky soil under foot, hostile governments in charge, and unfriendly neighbors on every border. Common people had little cause for gaity. That's why weddings were so important. They afforded a legitimate reason for a community to stop working to eat and drink and make merry for a few days. In a small town like Cana, where everybody knew everybody else, the whole village would join in the festivities.

Our modern weddings seem pretty tame when compared with these first-century fetes. We sit through a brief ceremony, congratulate the bride and groom, grab a little cake and punch, and rush back to work. We can scarcely appreciate the crisis we read about here. We would probably ask, "So they ran a little short of wine. So what's the big deal? The party has already been going on for several hours, or even days, so it should be winding down anyway, shouldn't it?"

19

We misunderstand. The guests are celebrating the happiness of the bride and groom, of course, but even more, they are celebrating life itself. These are ordinary people living ordinary lives, grabbing a chance to play for a change and to give thanks for the living of their days.

A man would endure drudgery for years to be able to provide enough food and wine for a week-long wedding celebration. If he should run short, he and his family—and the bride and groom—would suffer social humiliation that, in a small town with long memories, might never be forgotten.

Thus, when Mary whispers to Jesus, "They have no more wine," there's a touch of anxiety in her voice. She doesn't want her friends to be embarrassed.

Why does she tell Jesus? As He correctly points out, He really has no need to become involved. And what exactly does she expect Him to do?

John's brief telling of the story leaves several tantalizing questions unanswered. John doesn't bother with them, though, because in spite of Jesus' gentle rebuke, He does what His mother asks. He moves to prevent disaster for the hosts. The mother knows her Son.

His actions exhibit His power—quietly, without fanfare, and for what might seem, in light of the weightier problems He is to confront shortly, to be a frivolous reason. Why does Jesus take such pains on behalf of a social party? Can there be any other reason except His love for people? His miracle on this occasion proves that the Lord of Love wants His people to be able to celebrate life.

His love of people is the motive. We often see Jesus' love reaching out to the infirm, the insane, and the needy of all kinds, and we praise Him for His concern. We seldom include His miracle at Cana as an example of His love, however. The need of food, or of physical healing, or of emotional wholeness seems so much graver than the problem He addresses at the wedding that we may fail to appreciate what is going on here, with this apparently trivial use of His power.

But He obviously doesn't think the problem is trivial. That's because Jesus does not share the common opinion that the purpose of religion is to stamp out joy, or that God is some kind of nagging parent who lays down inflexible laws to keep us in line— and away from parties. Where did we get the idea that He is to be

20

served only with tears and moans and is displeased when we're having a good time? What a sordid, unscriptural, but altogether too typical stereotype of God!

I think God would have taken the side of a little boy in Canton, Ohio, that Mildred Welshimer Phillips used to enjoy telling about. His mother was a fearsome housekeeper, as strict a ruler in her domain as God is often accused of being in His, so strict that her husband and children wouldn't dare invite friends into the house—they might have ruffled a cushion or moved a chair! The house was a place to store and display furniture; the people were intruders.

No wonder the little five-year-old was surprised when he went over to his neighbor's house. As he started through the back door, he abruptly stopped because he noticed that the kitchen floor had just been scrubbed. Instead of scolding him, though, his neighbor called out, "It's all right to walk on the floor. Come on in!"

"Gee," he told her in amazement, "I wish my mother was as dirty as you are."[1]

Many people's religion is treated with the same protective care the little boy's mother lavished on her furniture, with the same negative effect on the people who live in it. They can't imagine the Lord laughing at a party, or doing His bit to keep the laughter of others alive. They have somehow missed the notes of joy that ring through the Scriptures. I wonder how they interpret these verses:

Praise the Lord.
Praise him with the sounding of the trumpet,
praise him with the harp and lyre,
praise him with tambourine and dancing,
praise him with the strings and flute,
praise him with the clash of cymbals,
praise him with resounding cymbals (Psalm 150:1, 3-5).

My soul *praises* the Lord
and my spirit *rejoices* in God my Savior (Luke 1:46, 47).

I bring you good news of *great joy* (Luke 2:10).

Then they worshiped him and returned to Jerusalem with *great*

---

[1]*Addresses* (Louisville: Standard Printing Company, 1967), p. 62.

21

joy. And they stayed continually at the temple, *praising* God (Luke 24:52, 53).

I have told you this so that my *joy* may be in you and that your *joy* may be complete (John 15:11).

So there was *great joy* in that city (Acts 8:8).

Far from the killjoy that His modern accusers charge Him with being, the Lord of Love promises that being His disciple is like participating in a perpetual wedding feast, with all the eating and drinking and dancing before the throne you can imagine (Matthew 22:1-14). The book of Revelation picks up this same theme: "Then the angel said to me, 'Write: "Blessed are those who are invited to the wedding supper of the Lamb!"' And he added, 'These are the true words of God'" (19:9).

His people's love for Him is reflected in these verses. Jesus' love of life is reflected in the delight people take in His presence. In the Gospel narratives, He is almost always surrounded by crowds who are there just because they enjoy hanging around Him. Whether He is healing or teaching or merely walking beside the sea, friends and foes alike are drawn to Him. Luke reports that several women support His ministry financially (8:3); he and the other Gospel writers take note of Jesus' special friendship with Mary, Martha, and Lazarus as well as the number of other homes that are opened to Him. His love for people is obviously returned with interest.

It is fascinating to observe the magnetic pull some charismatic personalities have on masses of people. I have been helped in my understanding of the crowds' affection for Jesus by observing some of our American presidents. I remember, for example, the extraordinary love affair between Dwight Eisenhower and his countrymen in the 1950s. Having now lived through several other presidencies, I still marvel at Ike's incredible rapport with crowds. Never one to "press the flesh" like some of our more traditional political leaders, the President nonetheless enjoyed a popularity that today's leaders would pay dearly to attain.

Journalist Theodore White, who has studied and written about America's presidential campaigns for many years, says he learned about president-watching from the Secret Service men who guarded them. They told him that the way to judge a crowd's feeling for a President is to watch the people *after* his car has passed them by. Crowds always smile and cheer as the President's car approaches, so their cheers don't mean very much. But if they keep on smiling after he's gone, that means they really love him.[2]

For two thousand years after Jesus passed by, the crowds have kept smiling. The Scriptures present a love affair between Jesus and His disciples so infectious that even over the distance of the years, we modern-day disciples have caught it. It is just as Aristotle said, "Nothing is so welcome to people who are in love as the sight of one another." You can't read the Gospels without observing how much Jesus and His followers enjoyed seeing each other.

I think of this often in our church's worship services. Some visitors must be shocked at the amount of laughter they hear. We don't apologize. In fact, we are almost boastful, because we are convinced that we worship the Lord of Love as much through our smiles and laughs as through our silence and prayers. Our cheerful hours together signal the security we feel in the presence of the Lord. The Bible tells us that the angels rejoice when a sinner repents—and we have no reason to believe that their rejoicing stops when they hear us singing and laughing with them. We have come into the house of the Lord to cheer!

A cheerless note comes down to us from the records of America's Civil War. The Fifty-fifth Massachusetts was encamped three miles from Charleston. On an expedition into the interior, it rescued and brought back to the camp about twelve hundred newly-freed slaves. A visiting Union officer was invited to address the freedmen, who shocked him by their haggard and forlorn appearance. He didn't know what to say to them, so he invited them to give three cheers for their new freedom. He started the yell, but they said nothing. He tried again, and yet again, but they couldn't respond. They had lived so long in slavery, the officer concluded, that they didn't know how to cheer.

Christians who have been rescued from their slavery to sin may sometimes be a little backward about cheering in the beginning, but our caution is temporary. When the full impact of our freedom in Christ makes itself felt in our lives, the only reasonable response is celebration. John speaks for twenty generations of

---

[2]*America in Search of Itself* (New York: Harper and Row, 1982), p. 44.

Christians when he writes (in 1 John 1:3, 4) that he wants his readers to know what he has seen and heard "so that you also may have fellowship with us. And our fellowship is with the Father and with his Son, Jesus Christ. We write this to make our *joy* complete."

So we Christians get together as often as we can, enjoying the sight of the Lord we love and of the ones we love in the Lord. Our worship is celebration.

Celebration of God

This is what makes Jesus so angry in the temple. Worship, the celebration of God, has been perverted. Money grubbers have turned the house of prayer into a noisy merchandise mart. What God intended for the benefit of His children has been allowed to degenerate into an efficient instrument for profiting from people's belief in God.

His actions here remind us of His anger in the synagogue in Capernaum (Mark 3:5) when He healed the man with a withered hand. His critics were ready to pounce on Him if He dared to perform a healing on the Sabbath. Their calloused unconcern for people's welfare grieved Him. Then, as now, He unleashed His power but, as always, His was power for the people, not against them.

Synagogue and temple authorities were the recognized rulers over their religious precincts, but it sometimes seemed to people that these rulers wielded their power against their subjects. Jesus, it seems, had no choice but to overpower them. The Lord of Love is always the champion of people's right to celebrate life and God.

Anger, even righteous anger, has such a bad reputation that I need to say a few words in its defense. A great deal has been written about its dangerous effects on the body. More than a hundred years ago, for example, a famous English doctor named John Hunter suffered a heart attack that nearly killed him. As a perceptive physician, Dr. Hunter knew the damage that negative emotions could inflict on him. "My life is in the hands of any rascal who chooses to annoy and tease me," he complained. And he was absolutely right, because in spite of his knowledge, he couldn't control himself. One day, in a fit of anger, he dropped dead.

At least he was honest enough to admit his infirmity, even

24

though he was too weak to control himself. Samuel Johnson, London's famous literary dictator in the eighteenth century, wouldn't acknowledge his. A well-known anecdote that has circulated for two centuries has the good man soliciting a parish minister's opinion of his defects. He said he wanted to mend them and ask forgiveness for them.

The minister rather frankly told Johnson that he was too hasty in his temper and very dogmatic.

This was more than Johnson was prepared to hear. "Dogmatic?" he huffed. "If there is one thing I am free from it is a dogmatic, hasty temper!" Then, purple-faced with anger, he ordered the frightened pastor out of his sight!

(What was it that Robert Burns asked? "Would some god the giftie gi'e us, To see ourselves as others see us"?)

Recent studies have proved that even in sports, the one area where a defense has traditionally been made for anger, losing one's temper does more harm than good. In the 1984 Winter Olympics in Sarajevo, Yugoslavia, Pat Ahern, the American champion in Nordic combined skiing, let his temper cost him a gold medal.

Here's what happened. Ahern leaped eighty-nine meters, making him a sure winner, except that the judges stopped the competition before the round of jumps had been completed. They inspected the course and ruled that all the jumps, including Ahern's eighty-nine-meter leap, had to be retaken. A restart for safety is built into the rules of international ski jumping, but the judges' decision caught Ahern by surprise.

What made matters worse is that this same jury had earlier disallowed an eighty-eight-meter jump by Ahern. Angry over what he considered unjust treatment, Ahern went ahead and jumped again, but managed to reach only eighty-three point five meters this time and, on the next day, managed a mediocre performance on the second part of the Nordic event, the fifteen-kilometer cross-country skiing contest.

Ahern was a far, far better competitor than his final effort showed. What killed his performance was his anger. Thomas Tutko, a psychology professor and cofounder of the Institute of Athletic Motivation, calls Ahern's a classic case of the effect anger can have on an individual sports performance. "If you get so mad that you'd really rather punch the judges, you're going to be off your game. Some athletes can channel the energy that anger generates to make themselves more astute and effective. But many of them have never developed that capacity."[3] So they lose.

Is there then nothing good to be said for anger?

Professor Tutko used the key word: "channel." Anger channeled, anger under the control of a higher purpose, can release energy and raise effectiveness. Anger in the cause of God can cleanse a temple; anger on behalf of people can set captives free.

Your early religious training may have been like some of mine. Even in a Christian college, I sat under a professor who dogmatically stated that anger is always evil. I have already admitted that most of it is, but to banish anger out of our system is to make ourselves less than human.

In so doing, we also deny something of the nature of God. In the Old Testament, there are more than 450 uses of the word *anger,* and 375 of them refer to God's! There are some things a holy God can't abide.

Our religious teachers, trying to steer us away from the dangers of uncontrolled temper, were properly motivated but dangerously misleading in their advice. What is needed is not the complete elimination of temper, but its control by a higher governing principle.

I like the confession of writer Evelyn Waugh (whose temperament should not be imitated). He confessed to a friend, "You have no idea how much nastier I would be if I was not a Catholic. Without supernatural aid I would hardly be a human being."[4]

Whether his Catholicism was sufficient to overcome his nastiness is open to question, but his tribute to the controlling power of religious faith is well placed. Jesus, who could be fierce when aroused, as exhibited in this temple episode, nonetheless earned a well-deserved reputation for His patience and mildness. His attack on the moneychangers was an exception to his otherwise gentle manner. But no one could ever accuse Him of being a Casper Milquetoast. He dedicated everything He had, including His capacity for anger, to the service of God.

In the Oscar-winning movie on the life of Mahatma Gandhi, the beneficial possibilities in anger are illustrated. Gandhi, whose life

---

[3]Edwin Kiester, Jr., "The Uses of Anger," *Psychology Today,* July 1984, p. 26.

[4]Quoted in "Waugh Stories," *Time,* December 8, 1975, p. 88.

was devoted to pacifism and self-sacrifice for his people, is remembered today as a patient, longsuffering gentleman. What many don't realize is that this pacifist was initially motivated by a burning rage. The struggling young lawyer was in South Africa in 1893, traveling by rail toward Pretoria. Gandhi didn't realize that he was violating any prohibition when he selected his seat in the first-class section, so when the train guard ordered him out of there into the baggage car, he refused to budge. Police were summoned, and they unceremoniously threw him and his luggage onto the train platform and left him there. He spent the night huddled in a corner of the waiting room, shivering with the cold—and with outrage.

By morning, his future course was set. He would fight for the rights of his people, no matter what it cost him. He was angry—but angry *for* his people. He would use every power at his disposal—but it would always be power *for* his people. He would channel his emotion in the way that Abraham Lincoln had earlier channeled his, biding his time, planning his strategy, preparing for the moment he could exercise his power *for* the slaves he wanted to set free.

Thus Jesus. For thirty years, He has lived quietly, biding His time, preparing for His ministry. Now He's ready. He celebrates life with the wedding party in Cana and then, offended by religious hucstering, He drives out the perverters from temple, the place to which people come to celebrate God. His joy in Cana and His anger in Jerusalem express His love *of* the people through His use of power *for* the people.

3

THE LORD LOVES YOU
AS YOU ARE

John 3:16, 17; 4:1-29

The world's favorite Bible verse is John 3:16: "For God so loved the world that he gave his one and only Son, that whoever believes in him shall not perish, but have eternal life." Even though many of us have memorized this unsurpassed statement, we may have missed how inclusive the love of God really is. A perfect, if somewhat surprising, example of how far God's love reaches is in John's next chapter, where we read of the famous conversation between Jesus and the woman at the well of Sychar.

The encounter is unexpected for several reason. In the first place, it takes place in Samaria. The location doesn't mean much to a modern reader, but most of Jesus' fellow Jews would have been not only surprised but offended to find Him there. Although Samaria lay between Galilee on the north and Judea to the south, thus being on the most direct route from one to the other, many Jews would cross the Jordan River and go the long way around in order to avoid passing through the territory of the hated Samaritans.

You have to know a little of their history to understand their prejudice. It began in 722 B.C., when the northern kingdom of Israel was defeated by Assyria. The conquering nation deported the Israelites from their land and resettled it with captives from other countries. These strangers brought their own gods with them and, in time, their worship became so mixed up with the worship of Israel's God that "purer" Israelites wanted nothing to do with them.

In 539 B.C. the descendants of Judah, the southern kingdom, began returning from their own captivity in Babylon. (The Babylonians had defeated Judah by 586 B.C.) They were dedicated to a strict observance of the Law—and horrified by the mongrel religion of the Samaritans. From then on, the hostilities were fierce. When Nehemiah was rebuilding the walls of Jerusalem, for example, the Samaritans did all they could to

29

stop him (Nehemiah 4:1, 2). Later centuries saw no letup of hostilities between Jews and Samaritans.

So the first surprise in this passage is that Jesus is in Samaria, speaking comfortably with a Samaritan.

A Samaritan woman, no less! That he is talking with a woman is the second surprise. It's a definite breach of accepted social customs. Men of Jesus' day, especially rabbis, do not speak to women without their husbands present. She's not only a woman, but the third surprise is the kind of woman she is. She's a sinner! Our first clue to her character—or at least her reputation—is the timing of her visit to the village well. She's there at the sixth hour (around noon), an unusual time for a woman to be drawing her day's supply of water. She has probably chosen this off hour to avoid meeting other women who would undoubtedly shun her since, as Jesus says, she has had five husbands and is currently living with a man outside of matrimony. She is not exactly the model of propriety!

This brief encounter bristles, then, with social dynamics: a Jew accepts a Samaritan as a social equal; a man engages in conversation with an unattended woman; a holy man respectfully listens and responds to a sinner's inquiries about God.

The woman is aware of the risks Jesus is running. She is surprised that He speaks to her, even more surprised that He is willing to drink out of her cup, and still more so that He promises her something He calls living water. Her surprise quickly yields to fascination, though, and her fascination to belief. She has never before met anyone like Him.

Neither have we. We call Him the Lord of Love because of His blindness to distinctions of race or religion or sex. Jesus, whose life defines righteousness, can still love the sinner whose life regularly does violence to everything He stands for—while we, on the other hand, who struggle so hard to keep our prejudices in check, hardly know what to think of His indiscriminate love. I'm afraid we might be as offended as Jesus' critics were if He were to display as little concern for our current social conventions as He did for those of His own people. What would we do if He insisted on treating women as completely equal with men? Or blacks as equal with whites? Or ghetto dwellers and "slum bums" as persons of as much importance as owners of country estates?

Could we be as free from prejudice as He?

In the racial turbulence of mid-nineteenth-century America,

Frederick Douglass rose to eminence as the leading spokesman for his black race. This remarkable fugitive slave from Baltimore saved his wages in order to buy the freedom of his childhood sweetheart, whom he then married and loved until she died years later.

After her death, Douglass remarried. The whole nation was up in arms over his marriage, because this time he married a white woman. White Americans poured scorn and contempt on him, and his fellow blacks called him a traitor to his race. They could hardly believe that he had so little regard for social customs governing relations between the races.

Douglass refused to repent, however. Instead of defending himself, he pointed to his mixed ancestry. "I do not see what they [my accusers] are troubled about," he said. "My first wife was the color of my mother. My second wife is the color of my father."

After Douglass was welcomed at the White House by President Abraham Lincoln, he later wrote in his essay about the event that in Lincoln's presence, he, Douglass, was color blind. He could accept Lincoln in spite of the fact he was a white man.

I tell this story because I am certain that many of my readers, perhaps you, will be bothered by it. We wonder whether colors should mix. We continue to be troubled by mixed marriages. What concerns me right now is not your position on this issue, but your feelings. If you are upset by Douglass' breach of social mores, you will then be more sympathetic with what Jesus' disciples felt when they returned from their shopping to find their Master sitting at the well talking to a woman, a Samaritan woman, a sinful Samaritan woman! They were shocked that He could accept this person that they all found so unacceptable.

Acceptance!

That's what this chapter is about, because acceptance is what love is about. Or at least, that's where love must begin. When the Bible says that God so loved the world that He gave, what He gave was acceptance.

The Lord of Love Gives Acceptance

To accept another person is to receive him or her without prejudice. That is, without pre-judging. Without deciding ahead of time whether the person is worthy of being invited into our presence. Without making the person fit into our categories of acceptability (what color? what sex? what background? what social

31

connections?). Without insisting that the person change to meet our expectations. ("I'll love you if you quit smoking, or stop being late for our dates, or improve your housekeeping, or stop seeing your old buddies.") Without waiting to see whether other people approve of our choice.

Our prejudices are so deeply rooted we can hardly function without them. They make life easier. They eliminate most of the human race from the list of persons we have to deal with. Jews don't have to speak to Samaritans nor Samaritans to Jews. Englishmen can dismiss Irishmen as beneath their notice; Poles can hold the Russians in contempt; the Japanese can disparage Koreans; Muslims can hate Christians; Hindus can hate Muslims; Protestants can revile Catholics; and Catholics can banish Protestants. It's all very simple.

We can go on. Republicans can dismiss all Democrats as reckless spendthrifts; Democrats can castigate all Republicans as greedy aristocrats. Teenagers can say all parents are old fogeys; those old fogeys can complain that all teenagers are juvenile delinquents.

There's more. All bankers are calloused, all lawyers are crooks, all preachers are hypocrites, all doctors are in it just for the money, all union leaders are gangsters, all chefs are drunks, all government workers are shiftless, all politicians are egotistical, and all blondes are dizzy.

But to nurture such prejudices demands its own kind of diligence. You have to stay alert, lest you find yourself accepting somebody you don't mean to, as did a woman who refused to take tranquilizers because, she said, "The last time I took them I found myself being friendly to people I wouldn't even speak to otherwise." You have to keep your guard up.

You and I may have to, that is, but Jesus doesn't. He has no prejudices to protect. He's the Lord of Love. He has been sent by the God who loved the world so much He gave His Son to make their eternal life possible. He loves the world's people just as they are.

And He doesn't love like the man who insisted, "Of course I love the human race. It's just people I can't stand." Jesus loves people. He loves individual persons. He loves this person, this woman, this Samaritan woman, this sinful Samaritan woman.

He shows His love by accepting her. He shows His acceptance by listening to her.

32

John has written his Gospel to give us Jesus' words, whose utterances are the words of life. But John also includes this woman's words as well, and to Jesus, they are important.

The Lord wants to help her, so He begins by listening, which is must harder work—and often a greater expression of love—than talking.

People sometimes take me aside and ask me to intercede for them with this or that person. They want *me* to talk and the other person to listen. "It'll do 'em good," they say. "They need to hear what you have to say," they tell me.

What these well-meaning folks fail to understand is that love demands more than talking. It demands listening. "I'm going to give him a good talking to," we parents sometimes say when we're upset with a wayward child. Wouldn't it be better, more often than not, to give him a good listening to? Love demands acceptance, and acceptance involves listening.

How many marriages have foundered because after the honeymoon, when the initial infatuation has worn off, husband and wife are too busy or too prejudiced or too selfish to listen to each other? So they grunt at the breakfast table, leave notes on the dining room table, and perform the expected rituals of kitchen and bedroom. But they talk without listening and cohabit without really communicating. Each insists on the right to talk but turns a deaf ear to the responsibility of listening. But Jesus listens.

And He makes requests. He compliments the woman by asking her to do a favor for Him. What a thoughtful, sensitive thing Jesus does here. Paul says in Philippines 2:5-11 that Christ Jesus humbled himself and became like a servant for our sakes. In His conversation with this woman, He shows the full extent of His humility. Here is the Son of God, asking a favor of a woman! That's acceptance.

I recently had a conversation with my "adopted" son Brian, which helped me appreciate what's happening between Jesus and this woman. Brian's money ran out before his month did, so he asked me for a little loan. I gave him the money, but felt it my fatherly duty to attach a little lecture to it, some things about thrift and advanced planning and Shakespeare's "neither a lender nor a borrower be" and other such pearls.

Brian was not totally appreciative of my thoughtful counsel. For one thing, he remembered an occasion or two when I had borrowed from him. For another, he felt the thoroughness of my lecture was out of proportion to the tinyness of the loan. Anyway, he hinted that he just might not ever borrow from me again—and made it sound as if his words were meant to be a threat instead of a promise.

They were a threat! His feeling free to ask me for a favor was a type of compliment, wasn't it? My wife and the rest of the kids do the same. Boy, do they! I in turn will ask for other special considerations from time to time. How can we do this? We do it because we feel so comfortable with each other, so totally accepted by one another, that we naturally turn here first for help. Our requests are signs of acceptance, indicators that we belong.

That's how much Jesus accepts the woman. There is no barrier between them.

In casually asking for a drink, then, Jesus begins to convey to the woman a touch of the love of God, for God so loves us that He accepts us, just as we are. We have trouble grasping this truth. We feel so unacceptable. Yet God's grace is vast enough to reach even to us.

In a famous sermon on the grace of God, Paul Tillich helps us to understand just how radical, how total, God's acceptance of us is, and how we are to receive it:

> "You are accepted, accepted by that which is greater than you, and the name of which you do not know. Do not ask for the name now; perhaps you will find it later. Do not try to do anything now; perhaps later you will do much. Do not seek for anything; do not perform anything; do not intend anything. Simply accept the fact that you are accepted."[1]

Tillich's insight is most appropriate for the discussion in Samaria, isn't it? Jesus doesn't ask the woman to do anything to gain His acceptance. He has already accepted her, as His request for the drink shows. She doesn't know Him yet, can't call His name yet, can't understand all He is saying yet, but she can, as Tillich says, accept the fact that she is accepted.

We sometimes find this hard, don't we, even in our personal relationships? How often a young lover has said, "I can't believe she loves me." Or an adopted child, after he finally believes that

---

[1]*The New Being* (New York: Charles Scribner's Sons, 1955), p. 48.

34

his adoptive parents really want him, marvels, "They love me. They really love me." That means, often, "They have accepted me. In spite of everything, they accept me."

The Lord of Love Gives Forgiveness

That phrase "in spite of" takes us a step further. Love involves acceptance, as we have just seen. What we may fail to grasp is that acceptance always includes forgiveness. John 3:*17,* which should always be quoted with 3:16, touches on this fact: "For God did not send his Son into the world to condemn the world, but to save the world through him." Why shouldn't He condemn the world? What has the world done to deserve being saved? Not a thing, yet God loves us anyway. He forgives us for what we have done, forgives us for being who we are. There is no prejudice in Him.

We have trouble forgiving people for being different from us, but God doesn't. He made us all, He loves us all, "red and yellow, black and white," thin ones, fat ones, short ones, tall ones. Tall ones. Short ones.

(Here I must pause to point out how much more gracious God is than human beings are. He is not prejudiced against short people. On a recent TWA flight, I was flipping through the airline's magazine and stopped to read a brief article that reminded me again of how much harder life is for us short people. A study of chief executive officers of Fortune 500 corporations found that more than half of those studied were six feet tall or taller. Only three percent, by contrast, were shorter than 5'7". I must protest. You know that all those tall people didn't get the chief offices because they were smarter. They were just taller, that's all. The world is organized to keep us short people down!)

To love is to accept is to forgive. I can't really love you until I forgive you for being who you are. Even if you are tall. Or short. Or cranky. Or reckless. Or a Samaritan. Or a woman. Or a sinner.

To love the world to me's no chore,
My big trouble's the man next door.

Jesus not only loves the world, but He loves the woman next door. He accepts her as she is. He implicitly forgives her even as He gently leads her upward.

Martin Luther King, Jr.'s words on forgiveness help us to see how Jesus is dealing with his new friend:

35

"Forgiveness does not mean ignoring what has been done or putting a false label on an evil act. It means, rather, that the evil act no longer remains a barrier to the relationship. Forgiveness is a catalyst creating the atmosphere necessary for a fresh start and a new beginning. It is the lifting of a burden or the canceling of a debt."[2]

The woman's lifestyle has been in violation of Biblical standards. Yet Jesus doesn't offer a word of condemnation. Everything in His manner suggests His readiness to forgive her for being who she is, even as He leads her upward to higher things. Jesus' love, in other words, is not dependent on her worthiness. Love is an attitude that is superior to our relationships; it dictates the nature of the relationship; it never allows the nature of the relationship or the character of the other person to dictate to it. In loving this woman, then, Jesus exhibits the love that God feels for us all, regardless of our status.

At the same time, He challenges us to put on acceptance and forgiveness, doesn't He?

Many marriages would be far, far better if husbands and wives could learn to accept each other genuinely, even to the point of forgiving not only what the spouse does but what the spouse is. Marriage counselors agree that couples must learn to accept each other's individuality and need for separateness, or mature love cannot flourish in their relationship. Family counselors add that parents must accept the fact that their children are individuals, also. They must not strait-jacket the youngsters into conformity with what the parents' have decided they should become; they must grant unconditional love, love that accepts and forgives differences. This kind of love does not drive children into good behavior; it lifts them to a higher level of living.

The Lord of Love Gives Us a Lift

The movement in the Sychar conversation is gently upward. What begins as a simple request for physical assistance moves upward to a question about proper worship and concludes on the highest possible note, a revelation of the nature of God. Jesus tenderly lifts the woman's attention from the mundane matters of everyday living to the possibilities of an abiding relationship with

---

[2]"Loving Your Enemies," *This Great Company,* David Poling, ed. (New Canaan, CT: Keats Publishing, Inc., 1976), p. 134.

36

the living Lord. Up to now her existence has been governed by her physical thirsts; Jesus offers her water from the well of eternal life. She has thought of God as residing in an earthly dwelling; Jesus lifts her to a vision of a God too great to be confined to a temple. His openness, His acceptance of her as she is, and His implicit forgiveness for being who she is free her to talk about what is in her heart of hearts.

She wants to talk about the Lord. She may be living in sin, but she is thinking of God.

Louis H. Evans tells of a woman who told her physician that she was on the verge of a nervous breakdown. Her temper was out of control, she was mean-spirited, and she was driving her husband and children away from her.

He examined her thoroughly, then told her she was organically perfect, although suffering from hypertension. His prescription, however, was somewhat unorthodox. He told her to get up fifteen minutes earlier ever day and spend that time reading her Bible for five minutes, then sitting quietly for five minutes thinking of what she had read, and then talking with God for the last five minutes.

She stormed out of his office, angry with his prescription and even more angry that he charged her fifty dollars for it. She hadn't gone to see him for spiritual advice; she wanted a physical diagnosis.

But she was pretty desperate, so she decided to try his prescription. At first, it was very, very difficult. But she persisted. Five minutes for the Bible, five minutes for meditation, five minutes for talking to God. After about two weeks, she noticed that her nerves were quieter and her temper much more patient. When she returned to her doctor, she said, "I feel well."

"You are well," he told her.

"What was the matter with me?" she wanted to know.

"My dear lady," he smiled, "you were simply God-hungry, that's all."[3]

The Samaritan woman quickly displays her God-hunger. As soon as she perceives Jesus' remarkable spiritual authority, she prepares to receive His wisdom. Such a person needs no scolding for her sins; she already knows them. She just needs an

---

[3] *Your Marriage—Duel or Duet?* (Old Tappan, NJ: Fleming H. Revel Company, 1976), pp. 50, 51.

opportunity to fill her hunger for God. Then she will rise above her situation.

When a group of Nazi prisoners arrived in Copenhagen at the close of World War II, there was a man at the station who kept shaking their hands and congratulating them on having survived Hitler's madness. "You are beautiful people," he repeatedly told them. "Ladies and gentlemen," he said, "welcome to Denmark."

One of the women couldn't take it. She knew how she looked and remembered how she had lived. She was a woman, all right, but she was no lady. "Lady? I'm not a lady," she protested.

The man said, "To me you are very much a lady."

"Look at me!" she must have fairly screamed at him.

"You are very beautiful," he told her, and kept on talking.

When he left, they found out he was the king of Denmark.[4]

The conversation was never forgotten. A king had called them beautiful. It made all the difference in how they saw themselves. A king had lifted them from the squalor of the concentration camp to acceptance as real persons.

"Come, see a man who told me everything I ever did. Could this be the Christ?" He has filled my God-hunger, He has treated me with love and acceptance, He has lifted my spirit. Could He be the Christ?

He could be. He is. And the Christ is the Lord of Love.

[4]Sylvia Rothchild, *Voices from the Holocaust* (New York: NAL Books, 1982), p. 183.

4

TAKING THE LORD OF LOVE AT HIS WORD

John 4:46-54; 14:23; 15:9-17

Jesus' reputation is spreading. You would expect Him to be recognized in Cana of Galilee, of course, since it was at a wedding here that He performed His first miracle when He turned water into wine. In addition, many Galileans were in Jerusalem for the Passover, so they had either observed or heard about Jesus' chasing the money changers out of the temple. The incident with the woman in Samaria had its effect also, since she broadcast her opinion that He was a prophet, or maybe even the Messiah!

People pay attention to celebrities, and Jesus is quickly becoming one. We are especially attracted to persons who can perform medical miracles. While He was in the capital city, Jesus effected many healings, and the word of these healings spread rapidly. One man in Cana listened with keen interest.

He is a royal official, probably a member of King Herod's court, assigned to duties in the province of Galilee. That's beside the point, however. It is in his more important role as father that he appears in this scene. He is the parent of a very sick son. With his official connections, you can be certain that he has already exhausted every source of healing for the boy, but without results. Jesus is his last hope. He begs Him for help.

At first the Lord of Love seems uncaring. "Unless you people see miraculous signs and wonders, you will never believe." Is He already tired of the demanding crowds? Is He disappointed because people seem so shallow? Or is he just testing the man's sincerity? If so, he passes. "Sir, come down before my child dies."

What Jesus does next tests the man's faith as nothing else could. "You may go," He tells him. "Your son will live."

That's all. He won't go with the official, and He won't talk with him any further. Yet He promises that the son will live. If you were in the father's place, what would you do? If you would refuse to return to Capernaum without Jesus or without some proof that Jesus had done something, you would be showing your

39

lack of faith in the Lord. On the other hand, if you would meekly walk away as He said, and on returning home you would find your son unimproved, you would look like a fool. What should you do?

He "Took Jesus at His Word"

The Bible says the official "took Jesus at his word and departed" (verse 50). When his servants meet him, he learns that the Lord of Love has kept His word. His son lives.

I have read this incident several times, but on this reading the New International Version's translation of one word helped me to see something in it I haven't seen before. The Greek word used in verse 50 is *episteusen,* "the man *believed* the word Jesus said to him." The more informal NIV translation packs the punch that got my attention: "The man *took him at his word.*" The phrase "take somebody at his word" holds together the elements of belief and obedience that faith requires. The man trusted Jesus enough to obey Him and go on home.

We are studying the meaning of love as we see it in the Lord of Love. Here Jesus teaches us love sometimes demands obedience.

This isn't the most popular aspect of love to talk about. Everybody likes to think of God as the God of love; the language gives us warm, cozy feelings about the deity. "God is love" is often translated to mean "God will put up with anything, because He is love. God won't judge, God won't condemn, and God won't get angry, because God is love."

How childish such thinking is becomes obvious to us when we think of a wise parent, who will *not* put up with anything *because of* love. Love judges, love sometimes gets angry, and certainly love sometimes expects obedience.

There's a kind of circular action here. Think for a few more moments about the love between parents and children. Love demands obedience, as we've said. Obedience, though, leads right back to love. Parents who expect their children to obey them enjoy a reward, because obedient children are more loving children. Love leads to obedience; obedience leads to greater love.

Two other passages in John illuminate this relationship for us.

"He Will Obey My Teaching"

"If anyone loves me, he will obey my teaching," Jesus says. "My Father will love him, and we will come to him and make our home with him. He who does not love me will not obey my teaching" (John 14:23, 24).

Here Jesus explicitly joins love and obedience with a reward, which is an intimate relationship between the Lord and His disciple.

Oswald Chambers comments that "we have to be so one with God that we do not continually need to ask for guidance. Sanctification means that we are made the children of God, and the natural life of a child is obedience." I like Chambers' insight here. A child who is close to his parents is not always asking what the parents want him to do; he already knows their will, and he wants to please them. The spirit of the parent, if you please, is one with the spirit of the child. They don't even use the word obedience, because what the child wants is what the parents want. The two wills become one. Love and trust and obedience are all wrapped up with each other.

They meet in the encounter between Jesus and the despairing father. His complete trust in Jesus enables him to take the Lord at His word. He has sought the Lord's help; now he accepts it on the Lord's terms.

How many of us would lead simpler lives if we could just learn this simple lesson. Loving the Lord means taking Him at His word! We accept His help on His terms. He's the doctor!

Dr. Paul Tournier of Switzerland complains in one of his books about the large number of patients physicians have to deal with who run from one to another to another, seeking medical advice from all of them but without completely obeying any of them. They "take delight in setting one against another . . . always looking for one that will allow what the other has forbidden . . . or exclaim, when one comes to the essential prescription, 'Ask anything you like of me, but not that!'"[1] I wonder whether this distraught father might have entertained such a thought, at least for an instant. "How can you ask me just to walk away? How can you expect me return home empty-handed with nothing more than your casual word that my son will be all right? You are asking too much!"

Surely he must have wanted some word of explanation: "You

---

[1] *The Healing of Persons* (New York: Harper and Row, 1965), p. 17.

41

may go home. Your son will be OK, because. . . ." But there was no "because."

One of the hard lessons for me to learn in my Christian life is that many of my requests for explanations are not going to be answered this side of Heaven. Fortunately, God does not demand that we completely understand His ways; He asks that we obey Him, not explain Him. "Oh, the folly of any mind that would explain God before obeying Him!" George Macdonald has written. "That would map out the character of God instead of crying, Lord, what wouldst thou have me to do?"[2]

Macdonald has come to the heart of it. God does not wish to enter into intellectual dialogue. He wants a loving relationship, like that of parent and child, and as Parent, He wants our full development. The mind is involved, of course, but more than mind; heart and soul and body and social life and financial well-being and everything else about us are the object of His love. Full development demands that we imitate Him, as a child imitates a parent (Ephesians 5:1). So when He tells us to follow Him, to obey Him, there is only one appropriate response.

"If You Obey, You Will Remain in My Love"

The second additional passage from John (15:9-17) makes this even more explicit: "If you obey my commands, you will remain in my love, just as I have obeyed my Father's commands and remain in his love" (verse 10). There's more, but let's pause here.

In the last chapter, I stressed the Biblical fact that the Lord loves us as we are. That's a fundamental teaching of the gospel. A second fact builds on the first one, though, and it also should never be forgotten. God does not expect us to stay just as we are. He wants His love to draw us upward to become more and more like Him. His commandments are designed to effect this upward pull.

A word of caution. We are talking about *His* commands, not the rules of churches or the laws of leaders. What I am saying in this chapter can be very dangerous if you equate the commands of the Lord with the dogmas of denominations or the legislation of church councils or the proclamations of preachers or the

---

[2] C. S. Lewis, ed., *George Macdonald, An Anthology,* (London: Fount Paperbacks, 1946), p. 89.

42

marching orders of militant popes. I can't forget C. P. Snow's observation that "far more, and far more hideous, crimes have been committed in the name of obedience than in the name of rebellion." History's religious wars offer too much proof that Snow is correct.

We are talking about obeying the Lord of Love. No one else.

"I have told you this so that my joy may be in you and that your joy may be complete" (verse 11). We need this verse, because it reminds us the Lord's commandments are for our benefit. He wants us to experience joy in life; He gets His joy from our joy. Once again the analogy of a loving parent comes to mind, doesn't it? Nothing makes parents happier than the happiness of their children. The commands they lay down for their children are meant to make their lives safer, happier, and more fulfilled.

That's what God wants for us. But we sometimes act as if we know better than He does. We devise little schemes to get around His orders, as Israel did in the days the nation had no king, when "everyone did as he saw fit" (Judges 17:6). We congratulate ourselves on our craftiness, only to find out when it's too late that we have only cheated ourselves.

A piece of Arizona history provides a case in point. Back in the 1870s, it was illegal in this state to sell whiskey to Indians. That little statute was a mere convenience, however. Ingenious Americans have never let an unpopular law stop them from doing what we want! There was a resourceful merchant up in Globe who found a way around the law. He began to sell potatoes for $2.00 apiece. Any customer buying one would receive a pint of whiskey absolutely free. In no time at all, the local Apaches bought up every potato the shopkeeper had in stock.

That presented another problem, but this time the Apaches showed their resourcefulness. They returned their potatoes to the merchant so they would be available for resale.

Everybody was happy. They found a way around the law. But you know the end of the story. The effect of "red-eye" on the Apache nation—and on the white settlers in this region—is too well known to need documentation here. The result has not been "joy."

Nor can we experience joy when we sneak around the Lord's commands. They are designed for our joy.

"My command is this: Love each other as I have loved you" (verse 12). This, then, is the command. Everything else the Lord of Love wants of us derives from this basic order: love each other. Now we come back to the royal official with his ill son. He takes the Lord at His word, and his son is healed. There is only one appropriate response to the Lord's command: we take Him at His word. When He tells us to love each other, we must love each other. It's not an option; it's a command.

Furthermore, He removes all doubt about the extent of the love. Lest we be unsure how much He has loved us and thus what is expected of us, He goes on to make His meaning explicit: **"Greater love has no one than this, that one lay down his life for his friends"** (verse 13).

First let me say a word about the nature of this love, and then a word about friendship. Earlier I pointed out that God doesn't want explanations, but obedience. This is why our response to Him must always be one of faith *and* love. It is possible to intellectualize faith, to treat it merely as mental assent to certain facts, and let it go at that (even though, from a Scriptural point of view, faith involves more than the mind). It is impossible, though, to intellectualize love. It involves feelings and actions as well as thoughts. A mind believes, but it takes a whole person to love.

Let me try to explain this negatively. I was stunned to discover that among the hated *Einsatsgruppen* commanders in Nazi concentration camps were many professional men—lawyers, teachers, artists, a physician, and, to my consternation, a clergyman. Even worse, these professionals earned a reputation for skill in bullying their prisoners and efficiency in killing!

I could hardly believe that a pastor was involved. We pastors have had specialized theological training. We learn the Bible in the original languages; we study the great systematic theologians. We are trained to handle the sacraments and to preach the Word. Our minds are fine-tuned to handle the jargon of our trade.

But there aren't any seminary courses for the heart.

Let me tell you about Ernst Biberstein. After being a Protestant pastor for eleven years, Biberstein entered the Church Ministry, a German state agency, in 1935. In 1936, he joined the feared SS. In 1940, he was sent to the Gestapo office in Oppeln where he helped deport Jews to the East. In the spring of 1942, he was sent to the field to conduct killing operations.

Americans learned about Biberstein at the Nuremberg Trials. He was one of twenty-two *Einsatzcommando* leaders tried there. Every one of them pleaded not guilty; not a one expressed regret for what he had done. When the president of the tribunal asked Biberstein whether, as a clergyman, he spoke any words of comfort or heard the last words of the Jews about to be slain, he answered contemptuously, "Mr. President, one does not cast pearls before swine."[3]

In his trial, Biberstein and others excused themselves from criminal culpability by claiming they were merely being obedient to their orders. Obedience. Yet here is a man who once claimed faith in the Lord of Love. And that Lord said, "My command is this: Love each other as I have loved you." In His love, He did not kill. He allowed himself to be killed instead. He laid down His life for His friends.

"You are my friends if you do what I command" (verse 14). Here is what the Lord of Love wants: not servile obedience, but active friendship. He hopes we'll be His active comrades in the cause of love. Then our lives will bear fruit.

The Lord loves us as we are, that was the point of the last chapter. But that is the love of a parent for a child, a master for a disciple. What He really desires, though, is more. He's after a reciprocal love relationship. As incredible as it sounds, the Lord wants us to be His friends! What begins with our obedience ends up in friendship.

Here's how it works. First, God loves us. ("This is love: not that we loved God, but that he loved us and sent his Son as an atoning sacrifice for our sins," 1 John 4:10.)

Second, we love God. ("We love because he first loved us," 1 John 4:19.)

Third, we love Him by obeying Him. ("My command is this: Love each other as I have loved you," John 15:12.)

Fourth, we love Him through obedience by loving each other. ("Dear friends, since God so loved us, we also ought to love one another. No one has ever seen God; but if we love each other, God lives in us and his love is made complete in us," 1 John 4:11, 12.)

Fifth, when we love as He loves and whom He loves, we cease to be just His children and become more like His friends. ("You are my friends if you do what I command," John 15:14.)

On May 24, 1950, a mother and her four-year-old daughter

---

[3]Nora Levin, *The Holocaust* (New York: Schocken Books, 1968), p. 245.

visited a friend who worked on a ship in the Brooklyn harbor. As they were boarding the ship, little Diana Svet fell into the narrow strip of water between the ship and its pier. Eighteen feet Diana fell, her mother screaming as she hit the water. Instantly 150 longshoremen who were unloading the ship sprang into action. They saw that if the ship drifted against the pier, the little girl would be crushed.

Nobody had to give them orders. They rushed to line up against the hull, pressing their shoulders against it with all their strength to keep the ship away from the dock.

Then three of them formed a human chain to save the child. Joseph Zapulla was the youngest, so he went down first. John Balzano seized Joe's ankles, then Guiseppe Sabino grabbed John's ankles and lowered his two friends down until Joe called, "I've got her. Pull me up."

Now four lives were at stake. All the longshoremen used all their strength to hold off the huge ship as the three men struggled. Guiseppe pulled with all the strength his powerful muscles could muster and slowly, inch by inch, he drew up the other two men and their precious treasure. Not until Diana was safe on the pier and started crying did the line of men step back from the ship. One of the guys remembered he had some milk in his lunch pail, and he gave it to the crying child.

Later that day, the newspaper called Joe, who was in bed with some minor bruises. They wanted his comments. He told them that the main thing was that the girl was all right. "I was just doing what I had to do," he said. "Why, it was all part of my day's work."[4]

That's right. Saving lives is all a part of our day's work. For Christians, there is no way around this. We have to take Jesus at His word. To love is all in a day's work. To love. To cooperate with other Christians in loving. In loving so that many lives can be saved. It's all in a day's work.

The church is a human chain working daily to rescue drowning children, and men, and women.

The church takes the Lord of Love at His word.

[4]Harold E. Fey in *The Christian Century*. Reproduced in *A Reader's Notebook,* compiled by Gerald Kennedy (New York: Harper and Brothers, 1953), p. 257.

5

LOVE ISN'T EITHER BLIND!

John 9:1-39

"How were your eyes opened?"

The neighbors had good reason to be curious. They had known the man from his birth and knew that his eyes had never been of any use to him. He had been able to scratch out his pitiful subsistence only by begging from his townspeople. Now they watched him watch them with eyes that could see. How was this possible?

If any single incident in the life of Jesus is a symbol of His effect on all His disciples, this is it. He makes the blind to see! These are the very words He uses, in fact, to define His ministry: "For judgment I have come into this world, so that the blind will see and those who see will become blind" (John 9:39).

"How were *your* eyes opened?" then becomes the question every disciple of Jesus loves to answer, for since He touched us, we can see as never before. Our experience with the Lord of Love offers us direct proof that, in spite of what the romantics of this world like to believe, love is not blind. To the contrary: the mutual love of Christ and His disciples *gives* sight; it reveals the truth that liberates. Love is what makes us see! "Truth cannot be had apart from love," Nels Ferre has written. "The loveless are blind. They are blinded by their own sin.... Love is blind only when it is selfish love, and that is no love."[1]

There is plenty of blind love in the unseeing man's life, but it isn't his. His parents, at least in this incident, protect themselves at his expense. They waste no time in separating themselves from the controversy swirling around their son. "He is of age; he will speak for himself. [We don't want to be involved. We won't get into trouble on his account. We don't know what happened to him and we don't want to know.] Ask him."

The Pharisees, religious leaders more accustomed to giving answers than asking questions, are so blinded by their love for their

---

[1]*God's New Age* (New York: Harper and Brothers, 1962), p. 71.

47

laws and regulations and their status as religious superiors that they can't see Jesus, and they won't see Him.

Only Jesus can give the blind man sight, and after He does, the man's vision keeps on improving. At first, all he knows is that "the man called Jesus" gave him his sight. Later, he realizes that Jesus is a prophet. Still later, he confesses his belief in the Son of Man. His insight increases in proportion to the growth of the prejudiced religious leaders' darkness of understanding. The healed man is the definite winner in the confrontation. In him, the truth of Jesus' words comes alive: "For judgment I have come into this world, so that the blind will see and those who see will become blind."

We admire the surge of power in the man. For years a beggar, he receives his sight and much, much more. Christ has infused him with courage; he is not afraid of the powerful Pharisees, and he will not be bullied into a betrayal of his Healer. He has been revitalized by the energy that the Lord of Love engenders. Leslie Weatherhead believes "a real experience of Christ which follows surrender, and loyalty to Him as far as one is able, is the most powerful force which the human personality ever knows and the greatest transforming energy the world has ever seen."[2] Weatherhead could have been writing about this formerly blind man who now bristles with new-found, Christ-inspired energy. He will not be intimidated. He sees the truth, and it has set him free.

The Pharisees refuse to accept the simple fact that Jesus has healed him. They are like skeptics of every age who fabricate any conceivable explanation to account for the sudden conversions Christ causes in lives. As a minister, I have had the thrill of being with men and women as they leave a wretched past for a wonderful future in the Lord. They are new beings in Christ! Then I have listened as pseudo-intellectuals have done their best to explain away the changes, giving credit to the most far-fetched explanations of the differences except the true one that the converts have decided, in faith, to let God take over their lives.

Malcolm Muggeridge has had the same experience. After living most of his long life as a prominent British journalist and celebrity, Muggeridge publicly confessed his conversion to Christ. He

---

[2]*Psychology and Life* (London: Hodder and Stoughton, 1934), pp. 127-28.

wryly commented ten years later that "one of the funny things about becoming a Christian in the twentieth century is that everybody looks around for some explanation other than the fact that one believes Christianity to be true, which, indeed, is the only basis on which anyone could become a Christian."[3]

Otherwise, why else would we put up with the criticism of intellectual or spiritual Pharisees? Wouldn't it be so much easier to go along with the spiritual temper of our times? It would, if we didn't have a conscience.

Conscience. If one's religious faith is genuine, it is here that he first feels its impact. Spiritual conversion immediately energizes the conscience. I have been bothered for a long time about Sammy Davis Jr.'s conversion to Judaism. I really don't want to believe the popular entertainer could have made the remark that has been attributed to him, but I haven't been able to forget it, either, because I'm afraid that it *is* the reason many people would honestly have to give for membership in their religion. The report I read stated that Davis' road to Judaism began with the accident that cost him the use of one eye. He said that was when he first learned to pray. Those first hesitant prayers then developed into a religious fervor that made him want to affiliate with an organized faith. All this is to the good. What bothered me, though, was the published account that said he was looking for an organized faith *that did not make demands on his individual conscience.*

If that is true, then he is to be pitied, because he may have settled for the form of religion without the reality of it. The real joy of religious faith is rooted in conviction. The truth is, if the Lord has made you see, really see, you have to make some choices. You have to do some things differently; you can't go on as you were. You can't be touched by the Lord of Love without having to decide between Him and the *status quo*. You will learn to see as He sees, with His much sharper distinctions between right and wrong, good and evil. Conviction sharpens conscience.

This is not just preacher talk. Here is the same truth spoken by one who saw the light for a moment, then decided against pursuing it. Lord Kenneth Clark, famed art historian and self-professed liberal humanist, disclosed in the second volume of his autobiography (*The Other Half: A Self-Portrait)* that he

---

[3]*Evangelical Newsletter,* November 18, 1977.

had had his own religious experience in the Church of San Lorenzo. There he was overwhelmed with a sense of heavenly joy that held him with unprecedented intensity.

I'm convinced the experience was genuine because of what he said it forced him to consider. It made him acknowledge that he was far from blameless and that if he were now going to be religious, he would have to reform. And, of course, there was no way his family would understand his conversion. They would think he had lost his mind.

After a while, the effect gradually wore off, and he did nothing to keep it from going. It was useless, he decided, to change his life; he was too much in the world to change course. Yet he recorded this extraordinary moment at the end of his life because, he said, it always helped him understand the joys of the saints. He knew their experiences were for real. He believed they had something that, for a fleeting moment, had been offered to him but that he could not pay the price to hold on to.

Christian discipleship does exact its price. That's the delightful testimony of C. S. Lewis, who has risen to preeminence among twentieth-century Christian writers. His encounter with Christ did not come as any kind of "religious experience" at all, but as the result of his unflinching, determinedly honest intellectual search. At one time, he proclaimed himself an atheist, yet he couldn't escape the God-question that kept haunting him. So he read—and read—and read, trying to justify his stand against God but increasingly doubting his doubts. Finally, as he writes in these frequently quoted lines from his autobiography, he gave in.

> "You must picture me alone in that room in Magdalen, night after night, feeling, whenever my mind lifted even for a second from my work, the steady, unrelenting approach of Him whom I so earnestly desired not to meet. That which I greatly feared had at last come upon me. In the Trinity Term of 1929 [when Lewis was 30] I gave in, and admitted that God was God, and knelt and prayed: perhaps, that night, the most dejected and reluctant convert in all England."[4]

He was reluctant because he knew the consequences. He could no longer hide himself in the libraries of academe. He couldn't be a disciple of Jesus in a closet. He would be laughed at, a particu-

---

[4]*Surprised by Joy* (New York: Harcourt, Brace and Company, 1956), pp. 228, 229.

larly bitter fate for a man who had himself scoffed at Christianity. He would have to speak his conscience. He had no choice, once he saw the light, but to tell what he knew about Jesus. "One thing I do know. I was blind but now I see."

On the way to the airport from a writer's clinic at California's Mt. Hermon Camp, my driver told me her remarkable conversion story. Her odyssey toward sight was not by way of intellectual inquiry, like Lewis', but along a sordid pathway that included alcohol, drugs, larceny, and illicit sex. She told me that she had been healed three years earlier, morally and physically.

She had been holding down two jobs. She worked full-time for the American Automobile Association and part-time for a twenty-four-hour convenience grocery store. And she regularly supplemented her income by stealing money from the grocery store. When the thefts were discovered, the company had employees take two different lie-detector tests. She passed both. Her employers thought she was clean. In the meantime, she kept drinking and popping pills. She also pursued her active lesbian love life.

Then came her hospitalization for a uterine operation. Somebody gave her a copy of Charles Colson's recently released *Born Again*. She was deeply moved by the account of his conversion and, there in her hospital bed, she turned her life over to the Lord. She confessed her sins and her crimes. She began repaying the money she had stolen and kept working until she had given back every penny. She received several promotions with the AAA. And, she told me, she is no longer gay. What she didn't have to tell me is that she is now a radiant Christian.

It couldn't have been easy for her to face her employers with the truth. Receiving Christ was no escape from responsibility for her, but a facing up to it!

In that respect, she is very much like a young man Peter Gillquist tells about in one of his books. Gillquist was present with a group of Bible-studying Christians one evening when a young college skeptic wandered into the group. He wore the uniform of the 1960s' rebellion: long hair, peace-symbol patches on his faded jeans, defiant expression on his face.

When he sat down, the contrast with the man next to him said it all. His neighbor was a middle-aged IBM executive, an officer in the Naval Reserve. He wore his conservative dark blue suit and closely trimmed, prematurely gray hair.

51

There they sat, the square and the rebel. But before the evening was over, the rebel capitulated. Sometime during the evening, he told the group, "something had happened" to him. He gave his heart to the Lord. Then he turned to the older man next to him and asked, "Would you come home with me?"

He agreed to go with him.

When they arrived at the home of the young man's parents, he got a flashlight and led his new friend and his parents to the garage, where he got a shovel and led them into the back yard. While the older man held the flashlight, the young man dug up hundreds of dollars worth of amphetamines he had buried there.

His parents watched in disbelief as their son systematically flushed the entire cache down the drain. People had suspected that he was a drug user, but no one had accused him of being a dealer.

That night, though, Jesus touched him and opened his eyes. Then he saw the sin in his life. He saw the ruin he was pushing on other drug users. And perhaps for the first time, he saw through a conservative dark blue suit and short haircut to the truthworthy Christian who wore them. When Jesus touched him, he turned with confidence to his new brother in the Lord. His so-called buddies in the drug culture couldn't help him find a new life; they had no life to offer. His Christian brother would accept him, forgive him, and walk beside him as he took his first steps in Christian faith.[5]

He knew he had to change—and he knew who would help him.

His is a happy story because it combines two essentials in spiritual rebirth: a desire to change and help to make the change.

If we have the desire, God grants the strength. When the people heard the first gospel sermon on the day of Pentecost, they asked the preacher, Peter, what they should do about their relationship to Jesus. He told them that they should "repent and be baptized." That would express their desire to be in Christ. Then he told them God's part: He would forgive their sins and give them the gift of the Holy Spirit (Acts 2:38). To their desire He would add the courage that comes from a clean conscience and the indwelling power of the Spirit.

---

[5]Peter Gillquist, *Let's Quit Fighting about the Holy Spirit* (Grand Rapids: Zondervan Publishing, 1974), pp. 123, 124.

The famous London preacher of a century ago, Charles Hadden Spurgeon, recalled his baptism as the moment he received God's strength.

> "To me, it is a solemn memory that I professed my faith openly in baptism. Vividly do I recall the scene. It was the third of May, and the weather was cold because of a keen wind. I see the broad river, and the crowds which lined the banks, and the company upon the ferry-boat. The Word of the Lord was preached by a man of God who is now gone home; and when he had done so, he went down into the water, and we followed him, and he baptized us. I remember how, after being the slave of timidity, I rose from the liquid grave quickened into *holy courage* [italics mine] by that one act of decision, consecrated henceforth to bear a life-long testimony. By an avowed death to the world I professed my desire henceforth to live with Jesus, for Jesus, and like Jesus."[6]

There is a sad note of a failure of courage in the *Diary* of one of America's early presidents. John Quincy Adams, who grew up in the shadow of his eminent father (America's second president), suffered throughout his lifetime from an unattractive personality. He agrees with people's opinion of him. "I am a man of reserved, cold, austere, and forbidding manner: my political adversaries say, a gloomy misanthropist, and my personal enemies, an unsocial savage. With a knowledge of the actual defect in my character, I have not the pliability to reform it."[7] Not totally blind, Adams could at least see that he needed to change. Partially blind, however, he could not see the Lord who makes His help available so we can change. Adams never felt the transforming touch of the Lord of Love.

Let me mention one more person who did. Some years ago, our country was shocked by the brutal mass murders that came to be known as the Sharon Tate slayings, since the famous actress was among the murdered ones. Charlie Manson and his so-called "family" of hippies were convicted of the murders. One of his followers, the chief murderer of the group, was Tex Watson, who later told his story in *Will You Die for Me?*

---

[6] D. O. Fuller, ed., *Spurgeon's Sermon Illustrations* (Grand Rapids: Zondervan, 1942), pp. 14, 15.

[7] Quoted in Harry Emerson Fosdick, *On Being a Real Person* (New York and London: Harper and Brothers, 1943), p. 60.

His description of his first months in prison is unforgettable. The killer who preyed on innocent victims was in turn preyed on by his overpowering fears. He had victimized others with his knife but was victimized by his hallucinations and finally, insanity. He imagined television cameras spying on his every move. He thought his food was drugged, he saw spies in dark corners, his hands glowed in the dark, and his memories of the screams in the night kept him from sleeping. The faces of the frightened people begging to be allowed to live appeared and reappeared day and night.

He was sent to the prison hospital, then released, then readmitted. His weight dropped from 165 to 110 pounds. They tied him down to the bed, and they jabbed feeding tubes down his nose; he thought he would drown in his own vomit. Psychiatrists watched him as he regressed into a fetal position, and they feared he would die before their eyes.

Then, from the deep recesses of his twisted mind, he began recalling words he had memorized years ago as a child. "The Lord is my shepherd; I shall not want." He repeated the Twenty-third Psalm over and over, all of it. As the words took hold of him, he became aware of another presence in the cell. Then he heard or remembered the words of Matthew 11:28, "Come to Me, all of you that are carrying burdens more than you can bear. . . . I won't turn you away." Then again the twenty-third Psalm, "Yea, though I walk through the valley of the shadow of death, I will fear no evil, *for thou art with me.*" No matter what.

There, a half-crazed, dying criminal felt the touch of the Lord of Love. He gave His life to the Lord, and the Lord gave sight to him. He saw the sinner he was; he saw the sins he had committed. But he also saw, as never before, that he was a human being created by God, loved by God, for whom God was eager to send rescue.

He wrote his book to tell the world that he's now alive, alive in the Lord, really seeing things clearly. He has been given his sight by the Lord of Love.

And His love isn't blind.

"For judgment I have come into this world, so that the blind will see and those who see will become blind."

54

6

LOVE GIVES IT ALL

John 10:1-18

The headline cheered: "He gave the ultimate." The subheading explained: "Hero passes up rescue line so others can survive crash." Pictures of the amazing rescue attempt dominated the front page.

Here's what happened. An Air Florida plane taking off in Washington, D. C., on January 14, 1982, clipped the Fourteenth Street Bridge and plummeted into the ice-clogged Potomac River, carrying seventy-six of its passengers to their deaths.

When the rescue helicopter arrived and threw down its flotation devices, the rescuers could spot only six survivors. Each time they tossed a line, the man who caught it passed it on to others, helping them to escape. When the rescuers returned for him after carrying the others to safety, they were too late. He had already slipped beneath the freezing waters.

A paramedic on the scene said he had never seen such commitment in anyone. He called him a true gentleman and hero.

Why did he do it? He did not even know his fellow victims, yet he laid down his life for them.

His remarkable heroism made the headlines, because this was not normal behavior. Your so-called "average man" would have fought to be the first one out of the water, instead of gallantly offering his place to others. The man's chivalry seems like something out of a nobler era. He acts almost like the Good Shepherd Jesus describes in John 10, the one who gives everything to protect his sheep. They seem to be worlds apart, don't they, this unknown hero in the Potomac and the gentle Shepherd in far away Palestine? But in this one thing, they come together: they know how far love must go.

No matter what words you use to describe them, victims trapped in surging waters or sheep endangered by thieves or careless hired hands, their plight is the same: they need to be rescued. They cry out for somebody who will love them enough to lay down his life to save them. That's how far love must go.

In Jesus' discourse on the Good Shepherd, it isn't only natural disasters like crashes and floods that threaten His people (the sheep). They are victimized by thieves and robbers who will sneak in among them to steal and kill and destroy. He probably has in mind the false prophets and messiahs who were crawling around Palestine in His day, exploiting people's fears and hatreds—just as they do now.

The sheep's safety is also threatened by the hired hands. A hireling is on the job for his pay. He doesn't love the sheep, but he loves the pay they give him the opportunity to earn by tending them. If any real danger comes up, he'll be the first to run off and leave the flock to their doom. Could Jesus be thinking of religious leaders here, men who should make the welfare of their flocks the most important priority in their lives—but don't? John Milton thought so. In the seventeenth century, the poet heaped scorn on traditional clergymen. They were nothing more than hired hands in his estimation. He called them "blind mouths," ignorant men more concerned with feeding their bellies than caring for the souls in their flocks.

By contrast, Jesus is the Good Shepherd. He knows His sheep, and He protects them at all costs, even the cost of His own life. In a delightful switch of metaphor, He calls himself both the Shepherd (verse 11) and the gate of the sheepfold (verse 7). The picture is this: at night the shepherd leads his flock to the protected enclosure. There he stands at the gate to inspect each sheep as it enters, looking for scratches or wounds. He anoints the wounds, waters the thirsty, and lends comfort to the sheep by his presence. Then, when they are counted and safe, he lies down to sleep across the doorway so that no one can leave or enter without disturbing him.

In his sleep as well as in his waking hours, he does everything for their sake. The Good Shepherd gives his all on behalf of the ones he loves.

In the Bible, Jesus is called both Shepherd and Lamb (1 Peter 5:4; John 1:29, 36). Both names remind His disciples that the Lord of Love sacrificed himself for our sakes. No matter how you define love, your definition must finally include sacrifice in its meaning.

He taught us by the way He loved us that when you truly love someone, you give it all. You are prepared to lay down your life for your beloved.

56

To Love Is to Do

The poet Rilke wrote in a letter to a young friend, "For one human being to love another ... is perhaps the most difficult of all our tasks, the ultimate, the last test and proof, the work for which all other work is but preparation." If he is right—and he is—it is because love gives everything, or it isn't love. This is what John Oxenham means in these often-quoted lines:

> Love ever gives,—
> Forgives—outlives,—
> And ever stands
> With open hands.
> And while it lives,
> It gives.
> For this is Love's prerogative,—
> To give, and give, and give."

And this is love's only prerogative.

It mustn't be confused with our ordinary acts of charity. It's much tougher, as Jack London points out: "A bone to the dog is not charity [love]. Charity is the bone shared with the dog, when you are just as hungry as the dog."

Love gives its all. Its ultimate demand was unforgettably dramatized for the whole world in World War II by Japan's suicidal *kamikaze* pilots. After the war, Americans got a better look at the planes these intrepid men flew against us. United States officials visited an aircraft factory about 70 miles north of Tokyo. There they saw the airfield lined with rows of single-engined fighter planes already rusting in the humid air. What most impressed them about these aircraft were the landing gears. The wheels were not retractable (so they could be pulled up after takeoff and dropped down into position for landing) but detachable. After takeoff, the pilot pulled a lever that, instead of pulling the landing gear up, dropped it off. It wouldn't be needed any more. The pilot did not intend to land his plane. He planned to die in it. These planes were designed for suicide missions. Every pilot knew when he entered the cockpit, he would not come out alive.

He was prepared to lay down his life for the country he loved.

His behavior still astonishes us. We're more accustomed to the easy morality of looking out for Number One. We can chuckle with the English M. P. Jeremy Thorpe who, after Prime Minister Harold Macmillan axed sixteen of his cabinet members in four days in 1962, observed cynically, "Greater love hath no man than this, that a man lay down his friends for his life." We expect a person to do whatever he has to to save his own skin. We really don't expect him to give his all for anybody!

Yet Jesus insists on a life of love and a love that sacrifices, as a shepherd sacrifices for his sheep. What impresses this writer is that Jesus says so little about religion and so much about love. I came into maturity in the fifties and sixties when religion was very popular in America. In the fifties, the more traditional Christian denominations were enjoying unprecedented prosperity. In the sixties, they fell on hard times but were quickly replaced in the nation's consciousness by a whole flood of cults and sects, many of them rooted in Eastern (that is, Hindu and Buddhist) religions. I remember Maharishi Mahesh Yogi, for example, who captured the spotlight when the Beatles and Mia Farrow and other celebrities became his disciples. He caught on very fast, and no wonder. He basically taught that man was not born to suffer and that he could escape suffering if he would just practice Transcendental Meditation regularly. It was religion without sweat.

Jesus talks about sweat. To be His disciple is to love one another, to love as He loved. And that means sacrifice. "I lay down my life for the sheep." "I have come that *they* may have life, and have it to the full." That is what love does—it offers up itself so that another may fully live!

To Love Is to Pay the Price

Jesus has already told us the price of love. It costs everything. Hired hands may run for cover, thieves may attack and steal, but the Good Shepherd stays and sacrifices. That is why the cross is so central to the Christian faith. The most obvious Christian symbol is the cross, because the most obvious Christian virtue is love. The cross of Jesus symbolizes the love of God in action. Jesus gave everything because God's love was ready to pay the price to save the ones He loved.

It is the price the Lord of Love expects His disciples to pay (John 15:12). We can't love each other with the attitude of hired hands. We adopt the spirit of the Shepherd toward all we genuinely love.

Let's see how this works. I learned something of the cost of love years ago in an extra-credit reading assignment I did for my senior English class in high school. From the teacher's recommended list, I chose to read Tolstoy's mammoth novel, *War and Peace*. Of

58

course, I read an abridged version. My teacher was still pretty impressed, though, that I would tackle such a large book even in its abbreviated form. That was my purpose for choosing it, of course.

It's a powerful book, and even then I could appreciate the author's genius. Much, much later, though, I came to admire the silent partner in Tolstoy's writing, his wife. When he was working on *War and Peace,* Tolstoy scratched out his rough draft by day, then in the evening, after she had put their child to bed and the confusion of the day had settled, Mrs. Tolstoy sat down at her table and, by candlelight, made clean copies of his rough drafts. She had to work for hours to translate his scribbling into a legible text. Then the next day, he would more than likely hand the same sheets back to her, covered with his corrections, some of them so small she had to have a magnifying glass to read them. Her son Ilya said in later years that she recopied most of the mammoth novel seven times. That's hard work. Yet she never complained. She was, in her way, sacrificing herself for her husband's career. She loved him, so she paid the price.

What Mrs. Tolstoy did for her husband is comparable to the sacrifices that people dedicated to any quest must be prepared to make. Earlier I mentioned the Japanese *kamikaze* pilots and their love of country. In America, we had a man who pushed himself almost to their extreme for the sheer love of flying. I am talking about Charles Lindberg, the first man to fly solo across the Atlantic. On that fateful day in 1927, when he had made his final preparations, having had only two hours of sleep before taking off, he said that when he entered the cockpit it would be like going into a death chamber. Stepping out of it in Paris, he added, would be like getting a pardon from the governor. He had already sacrificed greatly for the sake of his quest; he realized the enormity of the risk he was taking in the attempted crossing. There was every probability that He would even die. He was willing. He would do it for love.

What we must understand is the intensity of love's dedication. The object of the lover's affection may seem unworthy to an uninterested observer, but that doesn't take away from the fact that love pays the price. Philip Caputo, in *A Rumor of War,* his disturbing book on the Vietnam War, recalls Napoleon's boast that he could make men die for little pieces of ribbon. What brings Napoleon to Caputo's mind is his horror in discovering

59

that he would die for even less. During his training, he found himself so intent on receiving favorable remarks in his superiors' fitness reports that by the time his battalion left for Vietnam, he was ready to die for nothing more than their compliments.

Let me come closer to what Jesus has in mind. Most of us citizens of the industrialized West have trouble picturing the shepherd and his sheep out in the country. Let's imagine instead a loving teacher and his or her pupils. Think of the headmaster of a London school in the Second World War who, during an air attack, shepherded (this is the proper use of the word) all his children into the safety of the school's shelters. Then, going back one more time to make doubly certain that no one had been left behind, he was himself caught by a bomb and killed outright. He laid down his life for his sheep. He loved them.

He was doing for his class what Martin Luther thanked his parents for doing for him. Their sacrifice was not sudden death, but the daily offering of themselves in life-draining toil. The Luthers lived in tedious poverty. Of them Martin said, "My parents were very poor; my father was a wood-cutter. My mother had often carried the bundles of wood on her back, that she might earn something wherewith to bring us children up. They endured the hardest labor for our sakes." They paid the price of love.

What the schoolmaster did for his students and these parents did for their children, Jesus did for the whole human race. According to John 10:16, He loved those in His fold (an undoubted reference to His Jewish countrymen) and others not yet included (referring to the Gentiles to whom His disciples would carry His life-saving good news). It is a love so comprehensive, so all-inclusive, and so non-prejudicial that we can scarcely grasp its dimensions. Isaiah helps us come to terms with it in his great messianic prophecy:

> "Surely he took up our infirmities
> and carried our sorrows,
> yet we considered him stricken by God,
> smitten by him, and afflicted.
> But he was pierced for our transgressions,
> he was crushed for our iniquities;
> the punishment that brought us peace was upon him,
> and by his wounds we are healed" (Isaiah 53:4-5).

The Apostle Paul summarizes Isaiah's prophecy and Jesus' life when he writes in 2 Corinthians 5:21, "God made him [Christ] who had no sin to be sin for us, so that in him we might become the righteousness of God." The writer of Hebrews explains that "Christ was sacrificed once to take away the sins of many people" (Hebrews 9:17). The cross thus looms before us as the instrument by which Jesus took into himself the poison that was killing us, so that through His agony, we could live.

I read some years ago of the work of Dr. Claude Barlow, who, in a rare example of love of science and of people, imitated Christ's sacrifice. Whether he was consciously following Jesus, I don't know, but the parallel is there anyway. Dr. Barlow had gone to Egypt, where half of the country's 19,000,000 people were suffering from a dread disease caused by tiny parasitic worms called flukes. From the irrigation ditches of the Nile, he scooped up some snails that were infested with these flukes, bottled them, and brought them to America to study them in laboratories in this country. When he arrived, however, customs officials refused to allow him to bring them in. They were too dangerous.

What should he do? Without lab studies, all his efforts up to this point were in vain. Yet he couldn't carry the flukes into the country.

Yes, he could. There was one way, and he took it. He hid them in his own stomach.

He paid the price, too. His pain was excruciating, just as it was for the Egyptians. He suffered as they had suffered. The only relief he could get was from injections of tartar emetic, which left him nauseated for eight months. Just as it did the Egyptians.

Dr. Barlow made his body the laboratory to find a way to bring healing to the Egyptians. Remember Isaiah? "Surely he took up *our* infirmities and carried *our* sorrows. . . ." This is the price love pays.

There is no love without sacrifice.

Love gives it all.

7

THE LORD OF LOVE IS PRO-LIFE

John 11:25, 26

This is not a political chapter.

I am, though, borrowing a political word to capture the meaning of Lazarus' resurrection. Is there a better term for interpreting Jesus' statement to Martha than this one? Jesus is *pro-life*. He wants people to live. "I am the resurrection and the life. He who believes in me will live, even though he dies; and whoever lives and believes in me will never die." He wants us to live all the days of our lives and then, when those days are over, He wants us to live. The Lord of Love is pro-life.

In the Beginning of Life

I have borrowed the term *pro-life* from the current controversy over abortion. This complicated issue is often unfortunately reduced to slogans, one side insisting on a woman's right to do whatever she wants to with her body while the other side insists on the rights of the unborn fetus within the woman's body.

So the destiny of unborn babies has become the subject of a hot political issue open for debate instead of a settled moral and religious principle. This one, however, can never be resolved in a political party platform or by congressional vote. It deals with life and death; it has to do with the sanctity of human existence. This issue is bigger than politics—it is the essence of religion. If the fetus that results from the joining of egg and sperm is alive, then we are dealing with the mystery of human creation, and that is the indisputable arena where religion dictates to politics and not politics to religion.

In this arena, the Christian religion is pro-life. No, there isn't any verse that says in so many words, "Thou shalt not commit abortion." But the gospel announces in unequivocal terms the sanctity of human life and denounces man's propensity for devaluing that life. The world may consider human life of little consequence, but the Bible teaches that God created it and that He

63

valued it enough to send Jesus to rescue it, and He intended it for eternity. The arbitrary killing of unborn living human beings is an offense to the God who has created them.

The sexual revolution of the twentieth century, which has re-written the rules for male and female relationships, has had the unexpected result of cheapening human existence. It has urged us to become so pro-sex that we have ended up being anti-life. The method for reproducing life has become an end in itself; any unwanted consequences of our pleasure we casually kill.

We are reluctant to face up to the fact that a baby, even an unborn and incompletely developed baby, is more than flesh. It is more than egg and sperm. It is more than a happening taking place in a mother's body. It is no less than a creation of God, in which two human beings participate with Him to bring a new person into being.

If we consider ourselves mature enough to participate with God in conceiving a baby, then shouldn't we be responsible enough to assume the burden of the consequences? According to the psalmist, God takes personal interest in the conception and development of even preborn babies:

"For you created my inmost being;
    you knit me together in my mother's womb.
I praise you because I am fearfully and wonderfully made;
    your works are wonderful,
    I know that full well.
My frame was not hidden from you
    when I was made in the secret place.
When I was woven together in the depths of the earth,
    your eyes saw my unformed body.
All the days ordained for me
    were written in your book
    before one of them came to be" (Psalm 139:13-16).

The tender love of God for an unborn baby should come as no surprise to you. From the beginning, the Bible has taught that human beings are the supreme handiwork of our creative God. He has made us in His image. He has chosen to create us through the sexual union of male and female. When a man and a woman are joined in one body, and a baby is conceived, something sacred is the result. You don't treat the sacred lightly.

Even though modern science has taught us more about conception than our ancestors knew, we still find the miracle awesome.

And when we remember that God began taking personal interest in us in those dark months before we emerged from our mothers' wombs, we want to join the psalmist in singing,

> "What is man, that you are mindful of him,
> the son of man that you care for him?
> You made him a little lower than the heavenly beings
> and crowned him with glory and honor" (Psalm 8:4, 5).

Obviously, then, human life is not to be casually tampered with. It is God's. And if it is God's, then what happens in a woman's body is not the business of the woman alone. Nor of the woman and her man alone. It's their *and* God's business. He has made us, and we are His.

Let's put our views in this question into proper perspective. We have all been horrified by the slaughter of millions of human lives in World War II. Determined that such barbarity will never be repeated, we teach each new generation the terrors of Nazism. We've been even more astonished at the brutality of world Communism, which has been conservatively estimated to have killed at least 100 million people this century. Horrible, we cry. Butchers, we yell.

Yet the numbers of unborn babies that are killed by abortion every year in America alone is reaching into the millions. We seem oblivious to our inconsistency. The very people who castigate the Nazis and Communists for wasting human life will themselves callously snuff out a baby's life and consider themselves to be honorable citizens.

How shall we answer such people? What is the final word on the abortion issue? As far as I am concerned, this is it: our Lord is pro-life. In the beginning, when the baby is but a microscopic being, God is pro-life.

At the End, Also

When a person's days on earth are ended and his body has been laid to rest, our Lord is still pro-life.

When Jesus raises His friend Lazarus from his burial place, He makes God's statement on a subject that mankind has debated for thousands of years. Yes, there is life after death. What God has created, He intended to live longer than threescore years and ten. When the Lord created Lazarus, He designed him for a higher purpose than simply filling a tomb. He created him to live.

65

By raising Lazarus, Jesus turns Mary's and Martha's faith from the currently popular general belief in resurrection to a more specific trust in Jesus as the guarantor of life beyond death. "He who believes *in me* will live, even though he dies" (John 11:25). Martha has already confessed her faith that Lazarus "will rise again in the resurrection at the last day" (John 11:24), but Jesus helps her to understand that God has made Him the agent of resurrected life. "*I am* the resurrection and the life" (verse 25). A vague hope in life after death is not what Jesus offers, nor some fuzzy doctrine of reincarnation ("You'll have another life on earth after this one, as you have already had many lives."), nor even some universalist hope against hope that everybody everywhere will enjoy all the benefits of eternal glory no matter what they have believed or how they have acted or whom they have followed.

No, before Jesus raises Lazarus, He makes himself very clear: "I am the resurrection . . . Whoever lives and believes *in me* will never die."

There is life after death, and Jesus Christ is the way to it. "I am the way and the truth and the life. No one comes to the Father except through me." He tells His disciples later (John 14:6).

The apostle Paul believed this so strongly that he wrote to his friends in Philippi, "I desire to depart and be with Christ, which is better by far [than remaining here on earth]" (Philippians 1:23). Elsewhere he expands on this thought: "Therefore we are always confident and know that as long as we are at home in the body we are away from the Lord. We live by faith, not by sight. We are confident, I say, and would prefer to be away from the body and at home with the Lord" (2 Corinthians 5:6-8).

Paul experiences his body as a weight that prevents him from flying heavenward. He will remain in his body and serve his Lord as long as God calls him to do so, but his real desire is to die here so that he can live there in the immediate presence of the Lord. He values his life immensely, but his body he calls a "jar of clay" or a mere "earthly tent" (2 Corinthians 4:7; 5:1). He longs for the day that he can exchange his tent for "an eternal house in heaven." Life in this tent is often burdensome, and the tent itself is rent with flaws, but the new house, "not built by human hands," will be unblemished.

We shouldn't worry too much about this body, then, should we? Recently I visited a good friend whose "tent" is practically

66

worthless. Although only middle aged, she looks old beyond her years, and she fills her conversation with references to medical specialists of almost every description: immunologist, allergist, gynecologist, internist, ophthalmologist, and more. She is trapped in a body that continually malfunctions. It dominates her thinking and dictates her behavior.

God did not intend any person to be the slave of temporary housing. There is more to life than body. There is more to existence than this earth can hold.

One of my associates held a funeral service a few years ago for a man whom he had never met. When he went to the mortuary to meet the family, the deceased's widow was quite upset because the embalmer had done such a poor job preparing her husband for his burial. She kept mentioning little things that didn't look right. Finally she blurted it out: "It hardly looks like him at all."

Mike offered what comfort he could, but left feeling sorry for her and wishing he could do more.

More was done. When he returned the next day for the funeral, he was shown a completely different body. It seems that the funeral director had made a mistake. He had shipped the widow's husband to Kentucky and had a stranger's body in the casket the day before. They discovered their error in time to correct it for the funeral.

I suspect that had her husband been in the casket the day before, though, the widow still might have thought, "It hardly looks like him at all." Oh, the hair would be the same color and she could detect the same general features on his face and hands, but something would be missing. Something essential. It's called life. A body without the life is hard for us to look at. Figures in wax museums, no matter how skillful the artist who made them, seem—well, there is no other word, is there? They seem lifeless.

The apostle Paul, meditating on our life beyond the grave, contrasts our earthly body with our heavenly one. He says, "The body that is sown is perishable, it is raised imperishable; it is sown in dishonor, it is raised in glory; it is sown in weakness, it is raised in power; it is sown a natural body, it is raised a spiritual body" (1 Corinthians 15:42-44).

So we long for that new body, especially as we grow older, because our souls have outgrown our deteriorating bodies.

A. Kingsley Weatherhead's fine biography of one of England's leading twentieth-century preachers, Leslie Weatherhead, describes the older man's preparation for death—and life. He had achieved quite a reputation, not only for his preaching, but for effecting healing. Yet having been credited with assisting others to restored health, he himself suffered increasing physical disabilities with the years. He was attacked by chronic diverticulitis, he had numerous surgeries, he endured a chronic skin condition that required cortisone and ultraviolet light therapy. Insomnia troubled his nights, and anxiety haunted his days. By his seventies, he was tired of battling his body and he yearned toward death, where he would be rid of his aches and pains.

When he was seventy-five, he had a severe bout with peritonitis that nearly claimed his life. He wrote about it to his friend James Stewart as a "wonderful experience; as if one were in a field on a dull, gray day and then saw through a gate sunshine and happy people and incredible joy. I LONGED to go through the gate."

He said he prayed, as he had never prayed before, to die. But the doctors plied him with antibiotics, which hauled him back "with extreme reluctance." When his doctor told him, "I saved your life," Weatherhead asked him, "What for?"[1]

He had had a glimpse of his new life, and he was eager to go. He knew that the Lord is pro-life, even at the end.

And in the Living of Your Days

As God is in favor of life at its beginning and at its earthly end, He also desires that in the meantime we live all the days of our lives.

A T-shirt company recently sent me a brochure advertising an incredible assortment of their colorful products. Most of the shirts were stamped with eye-catching slogans. The one that held my attention the longest said, "Don't take life too seriously. It's not permanent."

That's just an upbeat version of an old, old philosophy. It's sometimes called *carpe diem,* which means "seize the day." Since today is all you have, since there isn't anything permanent about life, get the most out of the day while you have it. "Eat, drink, and be merry."

It's a good philosophy. I would quickly adopt it as my own, I

---

[1]A. Kingsley Weatherhead, *Leslie Weatherhead: A Personal Portrait* (New York: Abingdon Press, 1975), pp. 228, 229.

suppose, if I believed that life's not permanent. But I don't, so I can't. The Bible teaches that life *is* permanent; therefore the living of each day is serious business. (Not somber, mind you, or joyless—just serious).

Jesus tells Martha that He is "the resurrection *and the life*". He offers resurrection beyond the grave, as we have already noted. But He also promises life abundant now! ("I have come that they may have life, and have it to the full" John 10:10).

I have been a Christian so long I sometimes forget that Jesus' promise of a full life is not enjoyed by everyone. I was reading Isaac Bashevis Singer's novel *The Slave* when my enjoyment was halted by a character's definition of life. She is comforting her distraught husband with words that would have been anything but encouraging to me. "Do nothing, Adam," she says. "Go to sleep. Lie perfectly still with your eyes closed, and sleep will come. We must bide our time. Adam, dear, we must wait. What else is there to life? You wait and the days pass, and death comes and everything is over."[2] Is that all there is to it? Waiting and letting days pass and dying? Nothing more?

Methuselah lived 969 years and he died. Were all his days filled only with waiting and letting days pass and dying? What else would such a long life be except a living death? It was Seneca, wasn't it, who wrote, "Nothing is more disgraceful than that an old man should have nothing to show to prove that he has lived long, except his years."

I heard a speaker address a group of men recently on the subject of our human drives. He reminded us that our strongest drive is the urge to *live*. (Just let somebody hold your head under water and you'll see how strong it is.) The second is a need for *security,* the third the need to be *loved,* and the fourth a need to be *important.* He wasn't billed as a religious speaker, yet his topic is the very stuff of religion, isn't it? He was trying to help his audience define life. How to live it. How to make sense of it. How to succeed in it.

Successful living doesn't come easily, does it? You would probably agree with G. K. Chesterton, who grumbled that "the troublesome thing about life is not that it is rational or irrational but that

---

[2]*The Slave; Enemies, a Love Story; Shosha* (New York: Avenel Books, 1982), p. 101.

it is almost rational." It *almost* makes sense. Yet, when we observe the incredible stunts people pull in their frenzied attempts to be a success, we sometimes question their sanity, don't we? And then we wonder what they must think about us!

Life not only seems a little less than rational to us, it often appears almost criminal. From the backyard playground to the theaters of international warfare, human beings do everything in their power to hurt each other. You can easily sympathize with Bertrand Russell's conclusion: "Life is nothing but a competition to be the criminal rather than the victim."

How shall we live in these lawless, irrational days? Who can give us the knowledge we need to have live abundantly? The more we study, the more aware we become of our own ignorance, don't we? And the more ignorant we feel, the less capable we are of fashioning a successful life.

I have been sounding very pessimistic, but don't let me mislead you. If anything, I am a dedicated optimist. The source of my happy disposition is not my knowledge, however, nor my mastery of life's complexities, nor my being able so far to avoid the "bad breaks" that afflict so many people. My confidence derives from my firm conviction that Jesus *is* "the resurrection and the life." In *Him* is real living. He's pro-life.

When I was a college undergraduate, I first began thinking seriously about the difference Jesus was making in my understanding of life. I was studying *Antigone* by the great Greek playwright Sophocles. In the play, he includes a choral ode that sings the praises of man. He calls man the most awesome phenomenon. He drives his ships over stormy seas; he tills the earth with his plows; he captures the birds of the air, the beasts of the field, and the fish of the deep. He rules over the wild horse and the mountain bull. And best of all, he can speak and with his speech can fix his shifting thoughts and so found cities and civilizations. His power seems almost limitless.

There's that "almost" again. What keeps his majesty from being complete is that, in spite of all his strength, man comes finally to nothing. He can't escape or conquer death. He's trapped in his mortality.

That play was written more than two thousand years ago, yet its pessimism is as modern as the latest novels. In fact, when Graham Greene published his autobiography, he chose as his title, *Ways of Escape*. Life is something to be run away from, he implies. Many people, mourning the loss of their own lives, would deny that there is any way out for them. They are trapped by fate.

Against such fatalism Jesus stands. "No, you are not trapped," He shouts for all the world to hear. "I am the resurrection and the life." It is death that is powerless. Death cannot kill you. God made you to live. God has prepared an eternal home for you to live in. He's pro-life. He wants you alive, fully alive, forever.

And for now! If I believed with Sophocles that my earthly days were all I had, all I was ever going to have, then I wouldn't take life too seriously. I'd buy that T-shirt and go on my fling! But Jesus has made a difference. He has saved me from death, He has shown me how to live, and He has given me His Spirit to help me live every day to the fullest.

He wants us alive!

The Lord of Love is pro-life.

8

LOVE WASHES DIRTY FEET

John 13:1-17

Although Aleksandr Solzhenitsyn is a Russian, he has made himself the conscience of the Free World. For several years now, the exiled Soviet writer has fascinated the West, first through his powerful novels and memoirs with their outspoken criticisms of the Soviet regime, then through his equally blunt denunciation of the West's decadence and easy tolerance of evil.

He writes and speaks from a distinctively Christian point of view. He has suffered so deeply for his faith that he can't tolerate any pretense or posturing by Christian leaders.

That wasn't always true, however. When he was first arrested by Stalin's counterintelligence lackeys, Solzhenitsyn was a young Russian officer, proud of his rank, proud of his uniform, and very proud of his personal superiority. Even when they took him into custody, he could boast that he hadn't been arrested for stealing or treason or desertion. No, he was a prisoner of a higher type. He was being led away because he had, by his exalted reasoning powers, discovered the evil secrets of Stalin.

A man of Solzhenitsyn's superiority, he believed, should not have to carry his own suitcase into captivity. He was one of seven men who were arrested at the same time and, he quickly observed, he outranked the rest of them, especially the single German prisoner who was marching with them. So when his arresting officer ordered him to pick up his suitcase, he protested, "I am an officer. Let the German carry it."

And it was so. When the German became too exhausted to haul the Russian's luggage any farther, the other prisoners took their turns. All six of them lugged the heavy case. All of them but Solzhenitsyn. He was an officer.

Years later, he blushed when he reviewed the scene. He had walked empty-handed, congratulating himself on his superior rank and intelligence. But all the time, he was letting his work be done by others. He was so calloused, he added, that "if seven of us had to die on the way, and the eighth could have been saved by the convoy, what was to keep me from crying out: 'Sergeant! Save *me*. I am an officer.'"[1]

That's just how officers act, isn't it?

That's how the world in general acts as well, isn't it? "You know that the rulers of the Gentiles lord it over them, and their high officials exercise authority over them" (Matthew 20:25). That's just how things are. Generals bark at majors and majors lean on sergeants and sergeants make puppets of privates. Solzhenitsyn was just doing what comes naturally when he let the other captives bear his burden. He was an officer!

"Not so with you," Jesus commands. "Instead, whoever wants to become great among you must be your servant, and whoever wants to be first must be your slave" (Matthew 20:26, 27). This is what made Solzhenitsyn so ashamed of himself later. He had no right as a disciple of Jesus to think himself better than anybody else, no matter what his military rank. He was a Christian, and his Lord has turned the world's value system upside down.

It's a tough lesson for Jesus' disciples to learn. On the very night of their Lord's betrayal, for example, after the twelve disciples had been with Him for three years, they still had not caught on. Luke tell us that while they were eating, "a dispute arose among them as to which of them was considered to be greatest" (Luke 22:24). You wonder how they could have dared entertain such a subject in Jesus' presence, but such is the intensity of our need to be thought the best that we will squabble for preeminence even in the company of the Lord.

How does the Lord of Love deal with their pettiness? Luke says that he tried to make them understand that "the greatest among you should be like the youngest, and the one who rules like the one who serves" (Luke 22:26). But in the Gospel of John, Jesus does not rely on words. He acts out the humility He expects of His disciples. His example is a timeless reminder of a fact we all know, but choose to forget: love washes dirty feet. Without humility, there is no love.

Humility Expresses Love

"Having loved his own who were in the world, he now showed

---

[1]*The Gulag Archipelago* (New York: Harper and Row, 1973), pp. 165-167.

them the full extent of his love" (John 13:1). John is probably referring to the imminent crucifixion, which is Jesus' supreme declaration of love. But John may have the more immediate scene in view. The Lord's foot-washing service expresses His love, although it is so shocking to the disciples that they at first fail to see it for what it is. Here Jesus is as selfless in His love as He will be on the cross. When the Lord of Love stoops to the role of the lowest household servant, He is indeed demonstrating "the full extent of his love."

The towel and washbasin take their place with the cross as symbols of Jesus' utter humility. Paul says that Jesus "made himself nothing, taking the very nature of a servant. . . . [He] humbled himself and became obedient to death—even death on a cross" (Philippians 2:7, 8). The servant (towel and basin) and the savior (cross) are one in Jesus, because in Him, love finds its fullest manifestation. It is the same love that the Lord wants His disciples to express.

This is what took our Russian friend so many years to learn. He had not yet realized that as far as Jesus is concerned, the real test of our spiritual maturity is not, as we prefer, to rise through the ranks of religious (or any other kind of) hierarchy but, to the contrary, to descend to the role of servant. We prove our spiritual strength in the stuff of everyday life, where we bear one another's burdens in addition to our own.

I've been told that the root word of *humble* is the same as the root word of *human*. It is *humus,* earth. We are dust. All of us. No matter how many baubles we wear and of how many medals we boast, beneath the uniforms, we are all alike, all made of dust.

Yet this fact does little to make us humble. We still measure ourselves against each other, each trying to convince the other that "my dirt is better than your dirt."

You would expect that genuine humility would overcome us when we enter the presence of genuine goodness. That's what you would expect—but it's not what you get. Consider the audacity of the disciples, disputing about their own greatness while sitting at the table with Jesus. I guess it has always been thus. People who have the least cause to boast are also the least hesitant to congratulate themselves on their greatness.

Like *Hamlet's* Queen Gertrude, they boast too much, me thinks. They sound so full of themselves because they are so empty. They have to boast so loudly to convince themselves that

75

their words aren't ringing in a void. They can't be humble. They don't love enough. They especially don't love themselves enough.

Humility Assumes Confidence—in Self and in God

The biggest mistake people make on this subject is that of equating humility with lack of self confidence. They are afraid that to act and speak with confidence communicates arrogance.

They are wrong. Humility is neither weakness nor cowardice. Meekness isn't weakness. Only the truly confident have the courage to stoop to serve others.

Look closely at John's order here. First, he describes Jesus' absolute assurance of His relationship with God: "Jesus knew that the Father had put all things under his power, and that he had come from God and was returning to God" (John 13:3). This is John's explanation for Jesus' unprecedented behavior. It is as if John were saying something like this: "I know you will have trouble believing what I am about to tell you. It is extraordinary for a rabbi, or for anyone else as far as that goes, to get up from the table and voluntarily do the disgusting duties of the household's lowest servant. I want you to understand, though, why Jesus did it—and how it was possible for Him to do it. You see, He had such a good relationship with God, was so certain that He was doing the will of the One from whom He came and to whom He would be returning, that He could risk being misunderstood." When you know who you are, you aren't dependent upon status symbols or the rules of custom or the petty opinions of people who aren't as sure of themselves as you are. Jesus could wash feet because He knew who He was and because it is the nature of love to humble itself for the loved ones.

We all have a lot of fun joking about humility, I suppose because it is so rare an attribute among us. On my office door, a wag among my associates had tacked up a cartoon. It depicted the boss, sitting on his throne behind his huge desk, speaking down at his employee, "And, while it is only my humble suggestion, let's not forget who's the humbler and who's the humblee around here."

Our office gang gets a real kick out of these cartoons, usually at my expense. Another one appeared on the door one day. This was a *Frank 'n Ernest* strip. Once again the boss is behind his desk. This time a banner above him identifies the firm as the United Seafood Company. "Now don't misinterpret this," the boss says

76

to the exceptionally short man (Frank or Ernest, I never know which for sure) on the other side of the desk, "but I'm putting you in charge of the shrimp division." Why our staff thought of their diminutive pastor when they read this, I'll never know!

My family likes to get in on this act, too. For Father's Day this year, Kim gave me a memorable *Peanuts* greeting card. Lucy is speaking. "Dad," she says, "You're good-looking! You're witty! You're intelligent! And you're so talented!" So far so good. Then on the inside, "The family resemblance is amazing!"[2]

I don't think Kim was thinking theologically when she picked out this card, but once again Charles Schulz, the creator of these delightful *Peanuts* characters, has touched the truth with his humor. Here's where our confidence comes from. We're part of a superior family! We belong to the Lord. That means we have something to boast of—not our own attainments, of course, because they aren't much, but we can boast of the Lord, we can boast of the church, we can boast of the gospel, and we can boast of the love of the Lord. We certainly can't brag about our personal superiority, but we can point to the excellence of the faith we hold.

That faith, by the way, bolsters our sagging spirits just when we need reassuring. It tells us that God loves us, that Jesus sacrificed himself for us, that there is hope for us—even the likes of us! It assures us that God made us individuals, no two alike, yet every one important to Him. We applaud the little sixth-grade boy who understood this with the simplicity of a child. When his teacher asked the class to name something in the world today that wasn't here fifteen years ago, he answered, "Me." And the world is richer because he's here now. God put him here.

Do you see where humility comes from? It comes from knowing who we are, and why we're here, and where we are going. This knowledge keeps everything in perspective; it is the best antidote there is for swelled heads and inflated egos.

I was disappointed to read some things about comedian Jerry Lewis. As a boy, I laughed vigorously at the antics of this clown and his straight man, Dean Martin. Seeing their reruns today, I don't find the pair as funny as I did then, but in those days, I thought they were hilarious, especially the irrepressible Lewis.

_____
[2]United Feature Syndicate, Inc., 1952.

I was flipping through a magazine in a doctor's office recently, and in an article on Hollywood's starry "I'd" actors and actresses, I learned that when Lewis broke up with Martin, he announced that his goal was to make the world forget the great Charlie Chaplin. He said that out of 167,000,000 people in this country at that time, God had chosen *him* to make people laugh. He had to do it.

The same article said that Lewis has devoted a large room of his house to his library. That is not altogether unusual. What is unique, though, is that Lewis' library is lined from floor to ceiling by bookshelves stuffed solid with handsome books (bound in real leather) filled with clippings and pictures of Jerry Lewis.[3]

What motivates this driven man? There are probably many motives: a desire to lord it over Charlie Chaplin, a need to build up himself, a need to prove himself better than his background. Whatever else we may say, Lewis' comment betrays a failure to understand the will of the Lord of Love. I wonder whether he will succeed? How long do you suppose the world will remember the name of Jerry Lewis? I am reminded of Jesus' teaching that whoever tries to "keep" his life (whether he keeps it in leather-bound books in his library or however) will lose it.

We need to hear again Peter Marshall's famous prayer before the United States Senate, "We confess, our Father, that we know we need Thee, yet our swelled heads and our stubborn wills keep us trying to do without Thee. Forgive us for making so many mountains out of molehills and for exaggerating both our own importance and the problems that confront us."[4] We need to remember that truly confident and assured people know how to stoop.

Like Abraham Lincoln. There are so many examples of this great man's humility that we Americans constantly hold him up before our young people as an inspiring leader. We are equally touched by his wisdom in battle and by his gentleness in personal relations. A reporter once dropped in at the White House and was surprised to find him counting out dollars. Lincoln accounted for his unusual behavior by explaining that the President has many

---

[3]Helen Lawrenson, "Star Gazing," *Esquire,* June 1983, p. 174.

[4]Catherine Marshall, *A Man Called Peter* (New York: McGraw-Hill Book Co., 1951), p. 217.

duties beyond those spelled out by the Constitution and acts of Congress. He was doing one of them. A poor black porter in the treasury department was in the hospital with smallpox. He couldn't draw his pay because he couldn't sign his name. Lincoln had been going to considerable trouble, he said, to cut through the red tape between the man and his pay and, at last, he had succeeded. He was now dividing the money according to the poor man's wish and getting it ready for delivery.

With a war to conduct and a government to administer, he did not lord it over the lowly porter but instead humbled himself and became like his servant. He could do this, because he knew who he was. He did not have to prove himself important. He *was* important.

So was Jesus. He knew it. He also knew how importance must act, in the name of love. "Now that I, your Lord and Teacher, have washed your feet, you also should wash one another's feet. I have set you an example that you should do as I have done for you. I tell you the truth, no servant is greater than his master" (John 13:14-16).

We aren't. But our Master is great. Because of Him, we can serve with humility.

Humility Receives Its Own Reward

"Now that you know these things, you will be blessed if you do them" (John 13:17). This isn't Jesus' first offer of reward for humble behavior. He says something similar in the Sermon on the Mount. "Blessed are the poor in spirit, for theirs is the kingdom of heaven.... Blessed are the meek, for they will inherit the earth" (Matthew 5:3, 5). Blessed are those who don't push for special treatment; blessed are those who assume the servant's role; blessed are the humble.

Peter refuses to let Jesus wash his feet. He thinks it unseemly for the Master to act like a servant. "Lord, are you going to wash my feet?" (John 13:6). No way, Lord. Not my feet.

Jesus persuades him. "Unless I wash you, you have no part with me" (John 13:8). Scholars usually think this means that as Peter has to be washed in preparation for dinner, so he has to be cleansed by the Lord before he can enter into the Kingdom of God. The scholars are undoubtedly right, but they may be overlooking something else.

Jesus has promised that the humble will be blessed, and here He meekly asks to serve Peter. Unless Peter, with the same humility, allows His Lord to serve him, there can't really be any true fellowship between them. In his arrogance, he presumes to know better than his Lord. Real communion is impossible between them until Peter humbles himself just as the Lord has.

Now we come to the heart of the matter. We began by talking about love. We affirmed that love expresses itself humbly, and that it can only do so because true humility assumes real self-confidence, confidence rooted in God. Now we learn that humility has its own reward, and its reward is love, the kind of love that makes good friends, that makes fellowship possible. This is the love the apostle Paul refers to when he entreats Christians to prefer one another: "Love must be sincere. . . . Be devoted to one another in brotherly love. Honor one another above yourselves" (Romans 12:9, 10). The reward of honoring one another is that humility gives love a chance to grow.

When James J. Morgan became the president of the ailing Atari company, he showed keen insight into the rewards of humility. Atari was tumbling because it had bet so heavily on video games and sales were off badly. The fad was fading. But the real problem Morgan found, was arrogance. He announced that his goal was to make Atari "a humble company in the right sense of the word. Being humble in business means your customer is more important than you are."[5] You don't expect to hear this language in business, but Morgan is right. This kind of corporate humility has its own reward. (It may be too late for the once proud company. At this writing it looks as if even Morgan's skills won't be sufficient to save it. The humility needed to come sooner.)

You can apply it on a personal level as well. When the famous psychiatrist Dr. Karl Menninger was asked following a lecture on mental health what he would advise a person to do if that person felt a nervous breakdown coming on, he was probably expected to recommend a visit to a psychiatrist. Instead, Dr. Menninger is reported to have said he would advise him to lock up his house and go across the railway tracks to find someone in need. Then he should do something to help that person. Across the tracks—to someone "beneath" him. Become his servant. And thus recover his health.

---

[5]*Time,* February 6, 1984, p. 51.

Menninger must have learned this prescription from the Great Physician. It is the humility of love. It is the love of humility.

Humility is self-forgetfulness. Such absentmindedness is its own reward, isn't it? No one is more miserable than the person who thinks too much about himself. There is no cure for his sickness except in humbling himself to serve another. But this stooping is the source of personal power. No one is more powerful than he who has abandoned himself for the sake of a cause greater than himself. He will outperform any selfconscious person. He will ignore insults and threats and every obstacle. He will succeed. He will be free.

Freedom.

Success.

Power.

Fellowship.

Friendship.

Love.

These are the rewards of humility in love, of love in humility. Who could ask for anything more?

9

TO BE OR NOT TO BE

John 12:20-33

To be, or not to be; that is the question;—
Whether 'tis nobler in the mind to suffer
The slings and arrows of outrageous fortune,
Or to take arms against a sea of troubles,
And by opposing, end them?

Few lines of Shakespeare are better known than these. I remember a rowdy class of reluctant English students making great sport of them. "To be, or not to be," we declaimed with pear-shaped tones and lifted eyebrows, "that *is* the question." We knew the words. We just didn't realize awful relevance of their meaning.

If I had understood Shakespeare, I'd have been better prepared later when studying the works of the twentieth-century French writer Albert Camus. After staring hard at what he considered the absurdities of human existence, he concluded that there is only one really serious problem a human being must solve. He must decide whether life is or is not worth living. Should I or should I not commit suicide? "To be or not to be; that *is* the question."

Jesus raises the same issue in John 12, although from a different point of view. Suicide is not the question, but the meaning of life and its relation to death is. He turns a simple request for a visit ("Sir, we would like to see Jesus") into a probe of the reasons for His imminent death. He doesn't have time to chat with the Greek petitioners right now, because He is too busy getting ready to die.

He doesn't speak of that death as defeat, strangely enough, but as the supreme honor. "The hour has come for the Son of Man to be glorified" (John 12:23). With a characteristic reversal of human expectations, Jesus transforms apparent failure into God's triumph. Jesus claims that His crucifixion is victory.

In these few verses, the Lord of Love provides the divine rationale for His death.

83

To Succeed, You Must Be Prepared to Lose

We can hardly think of execution on a cross, a fate fit for criminals, as a way for the Lord to be "glorified." "Glory" conjures up visions of a regal coronation or an angelic anthem filling the heavens with majesty. At the very least, "glory" should refer to some revolutionaries' successful coup, like the overthrowing of the hated Roman overlords by someone like Jesus. It would never lead us to praise a crucifixion. You don't become a success by the way of a cross.

Yet crucifixion is exactly what Jesus is talking about. He must die in order to succeed. Further, He implies, this is the natural sequence in God's economy. In what really matters, to succeed you must lose.

For this to make any sense, though, we must first decide what we mean by success. Gary Bettenhausen will help us to define it. In an Indianapolis 500 race a few years ago, veteran driver Al Unser lost control of his race car, which then skidded into the track wall and exploded in flames. Seconds later, another driver slammed his vehicle to a stop and rushed to pull Unser out of danger.

That driver, Gary Bettenhausen, had been giving everything he had for months so that he would be ready to compete in the 500, but in a split second, he chose to let his chances die in order to save Unser. He failed as a driver. He succeeded as a man and friend.

Someone else won the trophy that day. It appeared that Bettenhausen lost. He considered himself a winner, though, because his friend was alive. That was glory enough.

In a less dramatic way, another man defined the meaning of glory for himself. According to Isaiah Thomas's history of printing in America, Benjamin Franklin had to come to terms with his convictions in the early days of *The Pennsylvania Gazette*. The struggling young publisher needed every penny he could get ahold of to keep his new paper alive, so when a man brought an article to him for publication, Franklin was eager to accept it. After quickly scanning it, however, the young publisher asked to be given a day to read the piece more thoroughly and make his decision.

When the man returned the next day, Franklin told him that he had found his writing scurrilous and defamatory. To help himself decide whether to run the article or not, he said he had purchased a twopenny loaf of bread at the baker's and with water from his pump had fixed his supper of bread and water. Then he wrapped himself in his greatcoat and lay on the floor and slept until the morning. For breakfast, he had more bread and water. He found that such a regimen did not inconvenience him and that he could, if necessary, live this way. He would not, then, have to prostitute himself by using his press to print articles of this kind. He reported his experience the next day.

He lost the man's patronage, but that was not as serious to him as denying his convictions. I don't have to add that his willingness to lose contributed to his success. No one would call Benjamin Franklin a loser.

I like hanging around with winners. They exude a vitality and optimism that is contagious. They seem to have excess energy; being in their company is like a battery recharge for me. I leave them with more zest than I had when I came to them.

There is something I have learned from them, though, and that is that almost all of these winners have lost at one time or another in their past. And, if necessary, they are prepared to lose again. Success is not so dear to them that they will sacrifice everything else for it. They are ready to lay down their achievements, if they have to, for the sake of what is even more important to them. They'll lose a race to save a friend.

Jesus' teaching in this passage flies in the face of the customary counsel of our age, doesn't it? "Watch your step," sages warn us. "He who fights and runs away, lives to fight another day." "Discretion is the better part of valor." You have these and similar bits of advice by memory, haven't you?

But more life has been lost in the cause of discretion, I suspect, than has ever been taken by recklessness. Timid souls who tiptoe through their days on earth exist by the millions, of course, but who can call this living? Far better to give the soul wings, to feel the thrill of challenge, and to run the risk of defeat.

The 1948 American Presidential race should have taught us something about the dangers of too much discretion. President Truman's upset victory over Governor Thomas E. Dewey was the biggest political surprise of the century. For years, pollsters and politicians have analyzed that campaign to find the secret of Truman's return to the White House. The best explanation I have found was offered by McGeorge Bundy, who was a chief aid to Dewey. He said that the Governor's strategists ran the campaign on the principle that if their candidate made no mistakes, he was certain to defeat the unpopular President.

So while Truman came out fighting, speaking boldly on issues, running the risk that he would offend the American populace even more than his outspokenness had already done, Dewey's camp sat around concentrating on making no mistakes. They succeeded in that goal. They were very discrete, the epitome of caution. But they lost the election.

It's all in the goal, isn't it? What is *really* important? Hanging on to your office, or your money, or your reputation, or even your life?

It was a question that William Larimer Mellon, Jr., asked of himself. He retired at thirty-seven, a man who had everything—good family life, all the money he needed, prestige in his community, and plenty of leisure. A success. But one evening he read the life of Dr. Albert Schweitzer, who turned his back on a brilliant career in theology and music to become a medical doctor in the Belgian Congo.

Mellon couldn't put Schweitzer's decision out of his mind. Finally he announced to his wife that he was going to enroll in medical school and settle down after that in some place that needed a good country doctor. He went to Tulane University and then moved to the country of Haiti, where he became the chief doctor of the first hospital in that area, built entirely with his own money.

By some people's standards, it was a foolish waste of his resources. He buried himself in one of the world's poorest countries, he squandered his substantial nest egg, he deserted his friends and loved ones. He gave up everything that America means when it says, "That's the life!"

Yet this loser comes out the winner when his life is contrasted with that of the middle-aged dentist Jim Conway writes about. He felt trapped in his profession, and he deeply resented the eighteen-year-old kid he once was for making the decision to become a dentist. "What I want to know is, who told that kid he could decide what I was going to have to do for the rest of my life?"[1]

His complaint isn't justified, though, is it? What welds him to

[1] *Men in Midlife Crisis* (Elgin, IL: David C. Cook Publishing Company, 1978), pp. 62, 63.

the dentist's drill, the boy's decision or the man's fear? He is afraid to lose his income, isn't he? Or afraid of what people will say if he gives up his profession, or afraid to change. Or afraid that if he tries something else, he won't succeed. So he goes to the office every day, curses his fate, and slowly dies.

He needs to listen to Jesus.

To Live, You Must Be Prepared to Die

"I tell you the truth, unless a kernel of wheat falls to the ground and dies, it remains only a single seed. But if it dies, it produces many seeds" (John 12:24). Jesus doesn't blink at the fact that He must give up His life. If He refuses His cross, His mission on earth fails. He will be nothing more than a footnote in history books, if that. Only His death can convince the world that He is, indeed, the Son of God.

Jesus is not speaking only of himself here. He has moved from the Son of Man to man. What is true of Him is true of all mankind. For us to live, to live as God means us to live, we must die.

Our concern in this book is love, and love doesn't bloom unless first there is a death, the death of one's dominating ego. If your ego comes first, then you won't commit yourself to anyone or anything else. You won't let anyone come close to you, because you don't want to get hurt. The self-protecting ego holds others at bay. It won't love, because it knows that where there is love, there is also pain.

That's why there can't be love without the death of ego. Ego protects itself so fiercely that it kills relationships, and life is found in relationships. But love reaches out, knowing full well it can be badly bruised but that it can never be destroyed.

You can count on it. If you reach out to another person, he may very well move away from you or turn you down or betray you or desert you. If you depend on him, you'll probably be hurt; if you sacrifice for him, he may take unfair advantage of you. But—if you are determined to keep yourself from getting hurt, you will die.

Let me return to Dr. Schweitzer. I mentioned that as a young man, he gave up his brilliant career on the organ and as a writer and teacher. It was a costly decision, and he paid for it. When on October 13, 1906, he sent letters to his parents and closest acquaintances announcing that he would enter Strasbourg University as a medical student to prepare for his missionary career, they were appalled. "You're like a brilliant general who exposes himself as a common soldier on the front line," one of his most valued teachers wrote to him. Most of his friends thought he had gone mad. One lady suggested that if he wanted to help the Africans, he could stay in Europe and give lectures and concerts on behalf of the natives there, and send the money to help them. That would be good enough.

Yet Schweitzer persevered. His correspondence shows that he was not blind to the possible consequences. There was every possibility that the diseases he was going to treat in that far-off land could attack and kill him. Then his long years in medical school would have been in vain. But he was ready to die.

God rewarded him with a life that has been celebrated all over the world.

The kind of sacrifice that Schweitzer was prepared to offer may not be required of all of us. Sometimes it is a simple matter of giving up an immediate reward in order to be true to our convictions.

Schweitzer must have readily identified with Jesus' words: "Now my heart is troubled, and what shall I say? 'Father, save me from this hour'? No, it was for this very reason I came to this hour. Father, glorify your name!" (John 12:27, 28). Again, Jesus refers to His death as a means of bringing glory. This time it is to God's honor. Verse 31 explains Jesus' words. "Now is the time for judgment on this world; now the prince of this world will be driven out." God has chosen Jesus' death (and apparent failure) to defeat His chief enemy. When Jesus dies on the cross, Satan appears to win. But appearance is not reality. God raises Jesus from the dead to prove that to die in the will of God is to live.

To Love, You Must Hate

The principles that I am finding in these few short verses of John 12 are really variations on a theme. Each is a different way of saying the same thing: "To succeed, you must be prepared to lose," "To live, you must be prepared to die," and, "To love, you must be prepared to hate," are facets of the same teaching. Each one forces a choice; it presses for a decision. Each requires a willingness to deny oneself in order to find oneself. "The man who loves his life [that is, who puts himself first] will lose it, while the man who hates his life in this world [that is, puts his interests last] will keep it for eternal life" (John 12:25).

88

Jesus has little use for exaggerated self-love. The me-first-ism so popular in secular society receives no encouragement from the Lord of Love. To the contrary, He teaches that we must "hate" ourselves.

This is a hard saying, but only because we misunderstand His meaning. "Hate" does not connote self-contempt; it is anything but suicidal. Jesus means that we need something or someone outside ourselves that means so much to us we forget all about ourselves, becoming indifferent to questions of personal comfort or security in our concern for another.

Jesus is the supreme example. He cares so much about completing His mission on earth that He lets himself be killed. That total commitment to God's will literally costs Him His life. It also saves it, as the resurrection proves.

There are many examples from Christian history of persons who have proved Jesus true. One of my favorites is William Wilberforce, the famous British Parliamentarian of the eighteenth century. As a youngster, Wilberforce was an indifferent student, wasting his way through Pocklington School, then through St. John's College in Cambridge. Upon the completion of his formal studies, he plunged into London's social whirl and entertained himself for three years in ways that he later deeply regretted. To other members of his crowd, however, he seemed quite the successful young man about town.

In 1784, he went to Nice, France, with Isaac Milner, an old friend who cared enough about him to ask what he was going to do with his life. Milner hated seeing a person of such potential wasting it the way he thought Wilberforce was. He admired the talents God had given his friend and wanted him to use them.

When they returned to England, Wilberforce handed himself over to God, for whatever purposes God could use him. Within just three years, he knew what God wanted of him. He would bring an end to England's slave trade.

It was an enormously expensive decision. He was single-handedly taking on England's most powerful businessmen and politicians. The leaders of the British Empire sincerely believed it could not survive without slave labor. The animosity Wilberforce called down on his head took him to the brink of death. No one was more devoutly hated. He could very well die in his struggle to free the slaves.

Then die he must. God had called him.

It took forty-six years, but God gave Wilberforce the victory. Twenty-two years before the United States emancipated the slaves, the British Parliament declared every slave in the Empire free.

It happened because one man was ready to die. Because he was indifferent to his own fate. Because he loved.

Like the Lord of Love before him. And, like Jesus, he has found glory.

Wilberforce loved God, so he loved what God loves and hated what God hates, things like selfishness, sinfulness, and our cozy but cruel disregard for injustice.

To Serve the Lord, You Must Follow Him

This, then, is the summary of the matter. "Whoever serves me must follow me; and where I am, my servant also will be" (John 12:26). Like Wilberforce before the English Parliament, or Schweitzer in disease-ridden jungles, or even Franklin preparing to live on bread and water, any disciple of Jesus follows his Lord and is faithful in His service, no matter what it costs.

This is true in big things, like slavery-fighting or jungle mission service, and in little things, like what happened to me just a few days ago. I shared my convictions on abortion—similar to what I said in the last chapter—with my congregation. As soon as I dismissed the worship service, several members accosted me in a good-natured but sincere way to register their disagreement.

I was sorry they couldn't share my convictions, but I assured them they hadn't offended me (although I seem to have done that to them). I told them they didn't have to agree with me. They aren't my disciples. But they are the Lord's. What matters—and it's a matter of life and death—is that they agree with Him. They must be certain that, in disagreeing with me, they are nevertheless agreeing with Him. It is always possible that I may be wrong, so they must never feel compelled to agree with me or with any other interpreter of God's Word. But their goal must always be to follow the Lord, no matter where He leads.

Following Jesus may lead to our own cross, a fact that He takes great pains to alert us to. We would rather not face up to it. I'm boasting these days about one of the young couples in our congregation preparing for mission service. They will leave us for Brazil, taking their three elementary-school children with them, much to the horror of one of their favorite relatives, their beloved Aunt

90

Fanny. You can understand her dismay, since she is far advanced in years and will be deprived of their company, although as it is, she lives in another state and seldom sees the family now.

She does write regularly, however, and she is not reticent in expressing her disapproval. She sends clippings of every newspaper article she reads that says anything negative about life in Brazil. She has warned them of the crime rate, the weather, the economy, and every other possible discomfort.

They are going anyway. They love Aunt Fanny, but they love the Lord more. They must follow Him.

They know that there is no real safety apart from Him, anyway. There is no other security.

One of the poignant stories to come out of the Nazi holocaust is of a father who went to Palestine in 1923 with the idea of buying some land and eventually moving there. He returned to Poland, though, because he didn't want to be the farmer he would be forced to become in the Holy Land. Their son had gone to Israel earlier, in 1919, and after working there for a few years, he moved on to Australia. His mother complained at length about his absence; she feared for his safety in the far-away lands. She was afraid she wouldn't see him again. After a while, her grumbling wore him down, and he returned to Poland where he married and had two kids. When the Nazis invaded, he was among the first Polish Jews to be killed.

His mother wanted him home where he would be safe.

There is no ultimate safety on this war-torn globe. Our only sanctuary is in the Lord.

So we follow Him—wherever.

10

UNAFRAID OF TOMORROW

John 14:1-7

When the TWA flight from New York to Chicago was hijacked to Paris by a group of Croatian nationalists, Edward O'Rourke, the Roman Catholic bishop of Peoria, did his best to minister to his fellow passengers. He refused an opportunity to leave the plane in Newfoundland, preferring to remain a captive in order to help the other captives.

Not everybody appreciated his help, however. Two passengers criticized the bishop later for frightening the passengers. And during the flight, an attendant upbraided him for "depressing" the people. His offense was in using the plane's public address system to urge the people to get right with God.

That seems like a reasonable thing for a religious leader to do, doesn't it? Yet some of the passengers apparently found his words frightening.

I wonder—were they afraid of his words or of their own spiritual condition? If you had been on that plane, would the bishop have offended you? Would your heart have been troubled, or would you have trusted in God?

"Do not let your hearts be troubled," Jesus tells His disciples in this famous passage from John 14. This is one of the two Scriptures I am most frequently asked to read at funerals, the other one being Psalm 23. Both encourage the believer not to be afraid of tomorrow, no matter what happens, because you can trust the Lord to take care of you, either as the Shepherd or the Way.

When Jesus first speaks the words, His followers need to hear them. They are very troubled. They can't shut their eyes to the threatening hostility of Jesus' enemies. In addition, He has just predicted that one of them will betray Him and another of them will disown Him (see John 13). He has further upset them with His unpleasant talk about His looming death.

They are troubled. It is beginning to look as if they have misplaced their allegiance. Everything seems to be falling apart. When they left everything to follow Jesus, they thought they were

93

joining a powerful new leader. For a while, their faith in Him was justified, thanks to His miracles and the incredible teachings and the great crowds. Even here in Jerusalem, His entry was something they would never tire of telling their grandchildren—palm branches waving, people's garments thrown on the road before their Master, the spine-thrilling shouts of "Hosanna" as He rode by.

But now it's Thursday, and the cheering has stopped. They are troubled.

We know what they are feeling. We have felt it ourselves. We, too, have given ourselves to the Master. At first everything seemed to be going our way. Then came the trouble.

Maybe it was the death of a dear loved one. You pray and plead and bargain with God, you give the best in medicine and personal care, you do everything in your power and ask for everything in God's, but death comes anyway. Your heart is troubled.

Word comes that there has been a terrible accident. Your heart is troubled.

Your children, over whom you have prayed so diligently and for whom you have willingly sacrificed so much, turn their backs on their childhood faith and follow the prince of this world. Your heart is troubled.

I remember a middle-aged man who made an appointment to see me at my church study. He lived in another part of our city but had been referred to me by a mutual friend. The man had been in our country for four years, having left his native India because he believed God wanted him to relocate his family in the United States. At first, everything seemed to confirm his decision. He had a good job in one of our town's large industrial firms. His wife and children were making a satisfactory adjustment to the strange ways of our culture.

Then his fortunes reversed. He lost his job in the general economic depression that had settled over America. No matter where he turned, he couldn't find work. He showed me his resume. His credentials were top-rate. Under ordinary circumstances, he should have had no trouble finding and keeping a job. He had turned everywhere, he said, but to no avail. His wife wanted to return to India, but he had no money to return and no money to remain. What should he do, he asked me. His heart was troubled, and he did not know where to turn. He was confused and had begun to doubt his ability to know the will of the Lord.

94

I remember that conversation as I read Jesus' words, because it symbolizes so many others. Like the first disciples of Jesus during this turbulent last week before His crucifixion, we latter-day followers of Him need to hear His comforting words. We are often troubled. What would He have us do?

His remedy is as straightforward as it can be: "Trust in God; trust also in me." Our hope in adverse circumstances is our faith in God. Jesus makes this even more concrete: You believe in God, in a Supreme Being who oversees your destiny. Become more personal with your faith—believe in me, the One the Father sent to you.

You Can Believe in Me—I Would Not Lie to You

"In my Father's house are many rooms; *if it were not so, I would have told you*" (John 14:2).

You can understand why Jesus needs to assure them that He's telling the truth here. If the first century was like ours—and in this respect it was—there were many self-proclaimed experts on the afterlife who made all kinds of promises regarding it. An ongoing debate raged between the Pharisees, who believed in resurrection from the dead, and the Sadducees, who did not, and claims and counterclaims flew between them.

You can hardly pick up a newspaper today without reading some of the same arguments. The height of absurdity was reached not long ago by a patient with a brain tumor in Ft. Lauderdale, Florida. Doctors had given him about four months to live, a fact he advertized in order to drum up customers for his new business. Not one to miss any opportunity, he made plans to take advantage of his condition. He offered to take messages from the living to the dead for only twenty dollars a message. Just in case anyone doubted, he said he would guarantee in writing that he would locate the deceased loved one after his own death and "spiritually" deliver the message. Some people believed him and forked over the money.

I wouldn't have.

But I do believe Jesus. The rest of the gospel record establishes His credibility with me, because He works so diligently to be certain that He never misleads us. He has been honest with us about all these things:

Persecution: "I am sending you out like sheep among wolves. Therefore be as shrewd as snakes and as innocent as doves. . . . All

95

men will hate you because of me, but he who stands firm to the end will be saved" (Matthew 10:16, 22).

Loss of comfort: "As they were walking along the road, a man said to him, 'I will follow you whereever you go.' Jesus replied, 'Foxes have holes and birds of the air have nests, but the Son of Man has no place to lay his head'" (Luke 9:57, 58).

Demands of discipleship: "If anyone would come after me, he must deny himself and take up his cross and follow me. For whoever wants to save his life will lose it, but whoever loses his life for me will find it" (Matthew 16:24, 25).

He spoke equally truthful words about Judas' betrayal and Peter's denial. His entire record bespeaks His integrity. When He speaks about life after death, then, we believe Him. He would not lie to us. (After all, He was staking everything on what He was saying as well.)

"*In my Father's house. . . .*" In speaking of God, Jesus chooses the most accurate human term He can find to express what God is like. "My Father has a house of many rooms, with rooms enough for you. I'm going away for a while. You'll call my absence death, separation; but I call it preparation, because I'll be getting your room ready for you.

"Then I'll come again, for you, and take you to be with me. Believe me. I would not lie to you."

You Can Trust Me—
I Want You to Be With Me Forever

"*. . . That you also may be where I am*" (John 14:3). I want our close companionship to go on and on. What we have begun on earth, we shall continue in Heaven. This love relationship must never be broken.

Here Jesus again speaks in very personal terms of God's great desire to bring His own back into His eternal embrace.

"For God so loved the world that he gave his one and only Son, that whoever believes in him shall not perish but have eternal life" (John 3:16).

"I know that his command leads to eternal life" (John 12:50).

"Jesus did many other miraculous signs in the presence of his disciples, which are not recorded in this book. But these are written that you may believe that Jesus is the Christ, the Son of God, and that by believing you may have life in his name" (John 20:30, 31).

Christians of all ages have held on to these and the many other Biblical promises that assure us of the Lord's desire to keep us with Him forever.

When my father died so suddenly at the age of seventy-three, a loving member of our church sent our family a sympathy card. We appreciated its thoughtful message, but we have cherished even more the note she enclosed in it. She told us that when her husband had died eight years earlier, she found comfort in a poem. She then thoughtfully copied it for us. It was a poem written by Edward Cane and entitled simply, "The Future." I'll quote the first two stanzas here, since they summarize so well the Christian's trust in the Lord, who wants us with Him forever.

> I know not what the future holds
> Of good or ill for me or mine
> I only know that God enfolds
> Me in His loving arms divine.
>
> So I shall walk the earth in trust
> That He who notes the sparrow's fall
> Will help me bear what'er I must
> And lend an ear when'er I call.

We can trust Him. He wants us to be with Him forever.

You Can Walk With Me—I Will Lead You

"I am the way and the truth and the life" (John 14:6). I am the way to God, I am the truth about God, I am the living embodiment of the life God promises and the means by which you can attain eternal life.

Jesus still has life after death in mind here, although what He does not say about it is as provocative as what he does. He offers no description of Heaven, prescribes no formula for attaining eternal life, and delivers no set of teachings to be mastered in order to gain entrance into the presence of God. He offers instead to be our guide.

This is a fundamental difference between the Old Testament and the New. After the giving of the Ten Commandments, as recorded in the fifth chapter of Deuteronomy, we read these words: "So be careful to do what the Lord your God has commanded you; do not turn aside to the right or to the left. Walk in all the way that the Lord your God has commanded you, so that

97

you may live and prosper and prolong your days in the land that you will possess" (Deuteronomy 5:32, 33). The way to God is through obedience to His commands.

The Lord spoke to Joshua in much the same manner: "Be strong and courageous, because you will lead these people to inherit the land I swore to their forefathers to give them. Be strong and very courageous. *Be careful to obey all the law my servant Moses gave you;* do not turn from it to the right or to the left, that you may be successful wherever you go." The Lord promises Joshua that if he will meditate on the law day and night and "be careful to do according to all that is written in it," then "you will be prosperous, and successful" (Joshua 1:6-8).

In the Old Testament, then, the law is the map that guides God's people through life. In the New, the map is replaced by a living Guide who knows the way and personally leads us.

I travel a great deal in other countries. Believe me, I know the difference between a map and a guide, and I much prefer the guide. I have been lost in more places than anyone else I have heard of. My friends know this about me, so they thoughtfully arrange to meet me at the airport so they can guide me safely around their countries. A map isn't good enough for me. I need a real person to show me the way.

God knows that about me and all the rest of the people like me, so He has sent Jesus to be the Way. He is with us now and will be with us forever.

Bruce Larson tells a delightful story of a first-grade class whose teacher, at the end of what was probably a very trying day, abandoned her lesson plans and drew her class around her in a circle for sharing time. She asked them to tell her what they wanted to be when they grew up. She heard the predictable: "I want to be a nurse like my mother," and, "I want to be a banker like my daddy," and even, "I want to be a teacher like you, Miss Smith." But when it came to be the turn of the shyest, quietest little boy in the class, they were all surprised by his dreams. He said, "When I get big, I'm going to be a lion tamer." He told them how he would work in a circus and would go into cages filled with ferocious lions and tigers with his gun and his whip and his chair. He'd make all those animals leap through hoops of fire and obey all his commands.

At this point, he must have noticed the wide eyes in that breath-

98

less crowd of first-graders. He realized what he was saying. "Well, of course," he quickly added, "I'll have my mother with me."[1]

The source of his courage was his mother; the source of ours is our Father and His Son. They are with us now; they will be with us in the future. The Son is the Way into that Future, so we have no need to be afraid.

He is also *the truth* (what He has spoken is the truth, what He has become reveals the truth—about God and man) and the life. Thus, in Him is our security. When we believe Him, we believe the truth; when we live for Him, we live life as God intended it to be experienced.

So we don't have to be afraid—of today or tomorrow. When Charlie Brown called on his psychiatrist, Dr. Lucy, she assured him that she never thought about the past nor worried about the future. But when he asked her about the present, she exploded, "The present drives me crazy!"[2]

She needs to hear from John Hendee, the Minister of Education in our church. His testimony inspires me every time I hear it. When John became a Christian as a teenager, the first challenge the Lord had to overcome in his life was his extreme shyness. He says, "I used to be so scared of people in any new situation, I almost threw up." John says that is not just a figure of speech; he became literally sick to his stomach, he was so afraid.

John is now one of the most effective evangelists I know. He has led more people to Christ than anyone else in our congregation. He looks forward to every opportunity to share his faith in Christ with anyone anytime. When you ask him what has made the difference, he will tell you, "I wanted to give my life to help others find what I'd found." That's it. The Lord has made such a difference in his life that he is eager to share the life-changing news about Jesus. Further, he has found that the Lord gives him the courage that he did not have before he gave himself to Christ. He is convinced that the Lord is with him now and that He will be with him in the future, so he is unafraid today and unafraid of tomorrow.

---

[1]Keith Miller and Bruce Larson, *Carriers of the Spirit* (Waco: Word Books, 1979), p. 200.

[2]Robert Shorts, *The Gospel According to Peanuts* (Atlanta: John Knox Press, n.d.), p. 78.

The Lord makes him secure. (This reminds me of a *Ziggy* cartoon someone left on my desk. It shows the little man gazing up at a plaque on the corner of a tall building. It reads, "These premises protected by a false sense of security."[3] Upon that insubstantial foundation all too many lives are tottering!) John trusts daily in the presence of the Lord of Love, who has banished his fear.

You Can Face Your Future With Hope

It isn't any wonder, is it, that Jesus' words in John 14 are read so often at funerals? For those who are in Christ Jesus, they offer assurance that we can face our future with hope. The Lord of Love has arranged for our eternal well-being. If we have known Jesus, we have known the Father and knowing Him, we have found the way to eternal life.

That is why we are unafraid of tomorrow. Do you remember the plight of Bishop O'Roarke, who was accused of frightening his fellow hostages? He is not the only one accused of disturbing the peace of people who are unprepared to meet God. In 1984, the National Federation for Decency published a news report that cleared up a puzzle for me. It concerned Billy Graham's film, "The Prodigal." I had been surprised to see that the film was given a PG (parental guidance suggested) rating. That made no sense to me, since that rating usually indicates the presence of violence or sex or profanity—none of which is in this movie.

The Motion Picture Association of America assigned the PG with this declaration, "Pre-teenage children should not be exposed to Christianity without their parents' consent." Why? What is there to be afraid of? Not a thing, unless you are scared of God! The Christian message preaches love, and perfect love casts out fear, even fear of death. Perhaps the MPAA is afraid of offending people, like the nervous flight attendant, by indirectly calling attention to their lack of preparation for the future, or by allowing the film to suggest that Jesus is the way through death to life.

The Word of the Lord is of a love that will not let us go, and that hope makes it possible for us to carry on. Charles Allen tells the moving story of a woman who had received the news that her son had been killed. She collapsed under the blow and went into her room, closed the door, and refused to see anyone.

---

[3]Tom Wilson. Universal Press Syndicate, 1984.

Ministers can sometimes walk where angels fear to tread, and hers entered the room and silently sat down by her bed. After a while, without any other words, he began softly and slowly repeating the twenty-third Psalm in the King James version. "The Lord is my shepherd, I shall not want." Phrase by phrase, line by line, he said the famous words. She listened.

Then as he continued, she joined in. "Yea, though I walk through the valley of the shadow of death, I will fear no evil, for thou art with me."

Her lips formed a small smile. "I see it differently now," she said. She could walk through her valley, she could face her future with confidence and hope, because the Lord of Love was with her.

He is with us, too, so we are unafraid of tomorrow.

11

HOW TO HANDLE REJECTION

John 15:18-27

I have been writing so confidently of the power of love that I may have misled you. If I have, it is time to correct the false impression. "Love conquers all," we like to say. We insist that there's no power on earth like love. But if we go beyond these assertions to expect our love always to be accepted and appreciated, we are in for bitter disappointment. To love is often to invite rejection.

In these chapters, we have been studying the Lord of Love in order to learn how to be His loving disciples. He has been teaching—and showing—us how to love one another and to love our neighbors as ourselves. So far so good. But what if our affection isn't wanted? What then?

The immediate impulse is to return curse for curse, rejection for rejection, hate for hate, in big things and in little. Just this morning, as I was out for a bite of breakfast before writing this chapter, I was informed of one of the members of my congregation who will probably be leaving us. She feels she isn't being spiritually fed. My preaching isn't deep enough.

She is rejecting me. I'm the teacher, and she thinks I'm not good enough for her. How should I react?

Nothing tests the mettle of our spiritual maturity more than having our love scorned. Everybody knows that "Hell hath no fury like a woman spurned." Women aren't the only ones spurned, though, nor are they the only furious ones. When our sensibilities are offended, we want to fight back, defend ourselves—get even!

This most natural inclination to salve our bruised egos slams against Jesus' most unnatural prohibition (at least we think it so). He has given His orders. He commands us to love. Everybody knows that. But what sobers us is what He promises will happen to us if we love with the love of the Lord. We'll be treated as He was treated. Our love, like His, will be despised. ("He was despised and rejected by men," Isaiah 53:3.) When it is, what shall we do? Jesus anticipates our problem. In this passage, He prepares us to handle rejection.

Remember Your Lord

Jesus begins with himself. We shall experience nothing that He hasn't already gone through. "If the world hates you, keep in mind that it hated me first" (John 15:18). From the moment of His birth, when a demented king sought to kill Him, to the darkness of Golgotha, when equally determined enemies succeeded in putting Him to death, the Lord of Love did battle with the harbingers of hate. He was the best thing that ever happened to this world, and we received Him in the only way we could. A hate-filled world cannot abide the presence of pure love. It will do whatever it must to snuff it out.

The world hated Jesus because of His teaching: "Remember the words I spoke to you: 'No servant is greater than his master.' If they persecuted me, they will persecute you also. If they obeyed my teaching, they will obey yours also'" (John 15:20). But they rejected His teaching, and they will reject ours as well.

Paul exhorts Timothy to "preach the Word." Then he adds realistically, "The time will come when men will not put up with sound doctrine. Instead, to suit their own desires, they will gather around them a great number of teachers to say what their itching ears want to hear. They will turn their ears away from the truth and turn aside to myths" (2 Timothy 4:2-4). Who wants to listen to the truth when it is so prickly? As Mark Twain's immortal Huck Finn concluded, "What's the use you learning to do right, when it's troublesome to do right and ain't no trouble to do wrong, and the wages is just the same?" People aren't going to welcome the teaching of Jesus or of any of His disciples. It's too troublesome.

The world hated Jesus in spite of His great works: "If I had not done among them what no one else did, they would not be guilty of sin. But now they have seen these miracles, and yet they have hated both me and my Father" (John 15:24). Think of it—He healed, drove out demons, fed the hungry, and did all manner of good among men. Yet they remained unconvinced. It is probably not overstating the case to affirm that they hated Him not only in spite of all the good He did among them, but because of it!

"That's not reasonable," we might protest. Jesus would agree. "They hated me without reason" (John 15:25).

When I am discouraged, I often think about how Jesus suffered at the hands of His enemies. Then I remember, "No servant is greater than his master." If, then, I am abused in my work for the Lord of Love, why should I be surprised? Hasn't He warned me? "If they persecuted me, they will persecute you also."

How did the Israelites treat Moses as he sacrificed everything to lead them to freedom? Did they shower him with praise and gifts of appreciation? Did they gladly follow his leadership? Did they agree with his teaching? No, they complained and fought and rebelled against and deserted him. What then should anyone who tries to lead others in the Lord's work expect? If an outstanding leader like Moses could not escape rejection, how can we?

Even the peerless apostle Paul was not appreciated. No one ever gave more for the cause of Christ than this remarkable man. Was he honored for his good work? Not to hear him tell it. "I have worked much harder, been in prison more frequently, been flogged more severely, and been exposed to death again and again." His enemies were not all outsiders, either. He says he was in danger from his own countrymen and from false brothers in the church (2 Corinthians 11:23f). If anyone should have enjoyed the universal goodwill of the early church, it was Paul. Yet his love was often rejected.

This lesson of public renunciation is one that political as well as religious leaders of all times have had to learn. When my family and I lived in Tennessee, we found out a little more about one of America's more unpopular presidents. Andrew Johnson went to Washington from Greenville, having had a most successful political career in the Volunteer State, capped by two terms as its governor. I already knew of his turbulent years in the White House following Abraham Lincoln's assassination, when a hostile Congress came within a breath of driving him from office. What I hadn't heard before was that the rejection he faced in Washington he had already experienced in his home state. In 1862, the Tennessee legislature declared Johnson an "alien enemy." His property was seized, and his house was made into a rebel hospital. He who had once been among the most popular citizens of his state was no longer welcome in its borders.

Passions were running high in 1862. Tennessee had declared for the confederacy, but Johnson joined many of his fellow East Tennesseans in loyalty to the union. Because of this political division, the state declared one of its most faithful servants an

105

enemy. He had chosen the wrong side, and the other side got even.

That's what happened to Jesus. He chose the wrong side. The devil offered Him all the kingdoms of this world if the Lord would just choose to worship him, but Jesus refused. So the devil's world got even.

We have made the same decision as Jesus, so we shall be dealt with also.

Remember: You Made Your Choice

"If you belonged to the world, it would love you as its own. As it is, you do not belong to the world, but I have chosen you out of the world. That is why the world hates you" (John 15:19). You can't have it both ways. You can't belong to Christ and at the same time be fully acceptable to the world that wants nothing to do with Him or His. When you became a Christian, you turned your back on the world. You judged the world and found it wanting. You can't expect it to be thrilled with your decision. When Christ called you out of the world, you accepted. You have jilted the world. It will get even.

I mentioned Huckleberry Finn before. Let me return to him for a moment, because I admire the precocious wisdom of Twain's remarkable character. Late in this justly famous novel, Huck has to make the toughest decision of his life. He and his friend, the runaway slave Jim, have completed their journey down the Mississippi on a raft. Jim has been captured, and Huck writes a letter to Miss Watson, Jim's owner, to tell her where he can be reclaimed. Then Huck gets to thinking about Jim, how good he has been to Huck, how he loves his family, and what a decent human being he is, even if he is black.

Huck knows he has to make a decision. If he sends this letter and Jim is returned to Miss Watson, Jim will spend the rest of his days as a slave. Yet if Huck doesn't betray his friend, he'll break the laws of his land and, he has been taught, the law of God. If he goes against what he has been told is God's law, he'll go to hell for it. What should he do? After a few minutes he sucks in his breath, tears up his letter and says, "All right then, I'll *go* to hell."

In the perverted ethic of that slave-holding society, Huck honestly believes that if he doesn't help send Jim back to slavery, he'll be committing the biggest sin of his life, and God will get him for it!

"It was awful thoughts," Twain has Huck tell us in the novel,

106

"and awful words, but they was said. And I let them stay said ...
and said I would take up wickedness.... And for a starter, I
would go to work and steal Jim out of slavery again; and if I
could think up anything worse, I would do that, too...."

What I admire about this young moralist is his courage to be
responsible for the effects of his choice. He is choosing to violate
society's laws. He will have to suffer for his choice. All right,
then, he will suffer.

Christians, we too have decided to live by a standard higher
than the laws of our land. We have given the cold shoulder to the
prince of this world and promised our allegiance to the Prince of
Heaven. We have set ourselves at odds with our times. What
should we expect from the world, whose ways we have turned
away from? We can't expect of this relationship anything more
than what Robert Frost said he had, "a lover's quarrel with the
world."

Let the Lord Help You

"When the Counselor comes, whom I will send to you from the
Father, the Spirit of truth who goes out from the Father, he will
testify about me" (John 15:26). The Lord of Love does not aban-
don us in our quarrel with the world. To the contrary, He fills us
with His Spirit. In the next chapter of John's Gospel, Jesus tells
His disciples that it is to their advantage that He is leaving them,
because then the Spirit (the Counselor) can take His place (John
16:5-15).

In our struggle to handle rejection in a Christlike manner, the
Holy Spirit plays a pivotal role. His job, as Jesus states it, is to
"testify about me." The Spirit holds us close to the Lord. He
reminds us who Jesus is, what Jesus did, what Jesus taught, and
what Jesus expects from His disciples.

This is vital. Almost all of today's popular heresies claim to be
following Jesus Christ. Every denomination, every cult, every
sect, even an atheistic one, appeals to people by claiming that
theirs is the true understanding of Jesus. It is frighteningly easy to
be led away from the true Jesus to a false one. How can we know?

We can trust the inspired ("Spirit-breathed") information
about the Lord that the Spirit has collected in the New Testament.
("All scripture is God-breathed and is useful for teaching, rebuk-
ing, correcting and training in righteousness, so that the man of
God may be thoroughly equipped for every good work,"

2 Timothy 3:16, 17). The Word of God is the "sword of the Spirit" (Ephesians 6:17), providing all the data about Jesus that we need. Anyone who adds to or takes away from the Spirit's book about the Lord does so at his own peril. The Spirit inspired John to write an account of Christ that would enable his readers to "believe that Jesus is the Christ, the Son of God, and that by believing [they] may have life in his name" (John 20:31). There is a lot of confusion today about the role of the Holy Spirit. But of this there is no doubt: He points to Jesus, and He works for the unity of His people. Further, He produces those qualities in us that will enable us to be steadfast in our love, even when it is rejected. "The fruit of the Spirit is love, joy, peace, patience, kindness, goodness, faithfulness, gentleness and self-control. Against such things there is no law. Those who belong to Christ Jesus have crucified the sinful nature with its passions and desires" (Galatians 5:22-24).

If we heed the words of Jesus, then, and (1) remember the Lord's experiences at the hands of ungrateful people, (2) remember that when we chose the Lord, we rejected the world and have to expect to face the consequences of our decision, and (3) rely on the help of the Holy Spirit to keep us true to the Lord in spite of everything, then we will be able to keep on loving when our love is rejected.

Keep on Loving

This is the acid test of Christian commitment, isn't it? Can you continue to treat others with steadfast goodwill and concern, even when they reject you? Jesus tells His disciples that they must testify on His behalf (John 15:27) even though they can expect the same treatment He has received.

This is just a more specific application of Jesus' general commandment, "Love your neighbor as yourself." Elsewhere He charges us to love our enemies and pray for those who persecute us (Matthew 5:44). He commands this for the sake of the enemy and of the lover. Augustine, the revered early-church theologian, confided in his *Confessions,* "It is strange that we should not realize that no enemy could be more dangerous to us than the hatred with which we hate him, and that by our efforts against him we do less damage to our enemy than is wrought in our own heart."

Jesus challenges us to love, then, for our sake—but also

because He cares for our enemies also. Love them—no matter what you feel about them. Love them—and thus prove that your feelings don't have to boss you around any more. Love them—and experience the power of love to transform the lover. Love them—for their sake, for your sake, for God's sake.

And when they spurn your love, love them all the more. "Love is patient, love is kind. It does not envy, it does not boast, it is not proud. It is not rude, it is not self-seeking, it is not easily angered, it keeps no record of wrongs. Love does not delight in evil but rejoices with the truth. It always protects, always trusts, always hopes, always perseveres. Love never fails" (1 Corinthians 13:4-8). No matter how many times it is knocked down, it gets up to love again.

It probably seems inappropriate to talk about boxing in a book about love, but something I learned about Rocky Marciano sheds light on the persistence required to be Jesus' disciple. Red Smith wrote of Marciano that any decent boxer could outpoint him for a few rounds. A Jersey Joe Walcott or an Archie Moore could knock him flat—and did. But they couldn't make him stay down.

Smith asked Marciano what he thought when Jersey Joe dropped him. That happened when Walcott was the champion and Rocky Marciano was just a crude young challenger. Walcott knocked him down in the very first round.

"Funny thing," Marciano answered. "I didn't think anything when I was on the floor, but going to my corner after the bell I thought, 'Hey, this old man knocked you down. He might knock you down three, four times more tonight. This could be a tough fight.'"[1]

He didn't have any idea of quitting the fight. He would be "rejected" several times before he would win, but he would keep getting up. His love for boxing wouldn't let him quit.

What then will you do when your love is rejected? When you're knock about or knocked down? When you are hurt so badly you think you'll never love again? When you want more than anything else to get even?

You'll keep on loving.

Like Jesus, who was also knocked down. In fact, He was

---

[1] Red Smith, *To Absent Friends* (New York: Atheneum, 1982), p. 112.

knocked out. They buried Him. But God raised Him from the dead so that He could go on loving. "Father, forgive them," He had cried out from the cross. "Father, forgive them," He now cries out from Heaven. The cry of love. Never a curse, never a threat to bring the angels down from Heaven to crush His opponents, never a promise to get even.

Love just gets up and loves again.

That's how you handle rejection. You keep on loving.

12

LOVE REACHES OUT
AND HANGS ON

John 17:20-26

Suppose there was only one Christian in the whole world.

Suppose also that he was a true believer who loved one other person so much that he shared his faith with him and within a year was able to persuade him to become a Christian.

Then suppose the next year that these two Christians loved two other persons and persuaded those two to become Christians also. At the end of the second year there would be four Christians.

Let's keep supposing. If the same thing happened the next year there would be eight, and at the end of the next there would be sixteen, and then thirty-two and then sixty-four.

Keep on. Do you know how many years it would take, with each Christian persuading just one person a year, for the entire world to be won for Christ? Approximately thirty-two years. From the time of Jesus until now we could have converted more than five dozen worlds like ours.

Then why haven't we? How do we justify our failure to be aggressively evangelistic, especially when we remember that "evangelism" is "proclaiming the *good* news" of salvation in Jesus Christ. When you have something good to share with people, it's pretty selfish to keep it to yourself.

It's also pretty un-Christian! You can't be a serious disciple of Christ without sharing your faith, because Jesus takes it for granted that this is the one thing above all other things we will do. "I pray also for those *who will believe in me through their message*" (John 17:20). Whatever Jesus has told His disciples, He expects them to pass on to others so that in time the whole world can believe in Him and have eternal life.

Jesus' great pastoral prayer fills the seventeenth chapter of the Gospel of John. The Lord of Love never forgets that He has been sent by the Father so that people may know the love of God ("let the world know that you sent me and have loved them even as you have loved me," John 17:23) and receive eternal life through the

111

Son ("For you granted [your Son] authority over all people that he might give eternal life to all those you have given him," John 17:2). In this prayer, the Lord of Love teaches us that love reaches out and hangs on.

Love Reaches Out

The word we use in Christian circles is *evangelism*. As I already stated, it literally means proclaiming the good news of Jesus Christ. The Christian church's evangelism program was born in the heart of God, who could not stand to see men and women in darkness and sin, so He sent Jesus on a rescue mission with orders to save as many as would believe in Him. Jesus never forgets His calling. He prays to His Father, "I have brought you glory on earth by completing the work you gave me to do" (John 17:4). The saving work He began and personally completed through His death on the cross, He commissions His disciples to carry on until the whole world should turn to God (Matthew 28:18-20). He alludes to this commission in His prayer, "As you sent me into the world, I have sent them into the world" (John 17:18).

This part of His prayer has personal significance for me. When I was ordained into the Christian ministry twenty-five years ago, Jesus' words to His disciples were sung to me, "As the Father has sent me, so send I you" (John 20:21). My ordaining church sent me forth to save lives, nothing less. I was charged to remember that Jesus did not intend for His love to be felt by His closest disciples only. I must never forget that love reaches out.

That is why the Lord of Love established a church to expand His ministry after He left the earth. He intended it to be, as E. Stanley Jones has accurately named it, "a society of organized love." It's the body of Christ, loving the world now *as* His body the way Jesus loved the world two centuries ago *in* His body.

I like the way the Roman Catholic writer, Dr. Y. M. J. Congar, has explained the motive for the church's outreach: "The missionary torrent is a torrent of love, for the Father's sending the Son into the world is a deed of love. . . . The object of the Church's mission, is the object of Christ's, with this difference, that salvation has no longer to be purchased but to be communicated."[1]

---

[1] Quoted by Paul S. Rees, *Don't Sleep Through the Revolution* (Waco: Word Books, 1969), p. 34.

112

When you've been knocked over by a torrent, it's not hard to communicate a reaction! When you've actually received the love of God in your life, you have to talk about it. You can't keep the torrent confined—it flows through. The famous London preacher of a century ago, Charles Haddon Spurgeon, used another metaphor. When was asked how he could communicate the way he did, he answered, "It's very simple. Pour some kerosene over you, light a match, and people will come to watch you burn."

He was on fire with the love of the Lord. He couldn't keep from shouting to anyone in hearing distance that God so loved the world that He sent Christ, and that Christ so loved that He gave himself up for the world. When we love the Lord and love the Lord's world as Spurgeon loved it, we will do everything in our power to see that as many people as possible learn of and experience the love of God in Christ. God's love is a torrent that can't be stopped, a fire that can't be extinguished. It spreads from the heart of God through the sacrifice of Christ through the ministry of Christians to anybody who hasn't felt it yet.

Love moves us to action. Literally. I am thinking of Ona Liles, crying over homeless children in India, praying God would make it possible for him to move to that country to help them. God did not open that door but another, so the Liles are in Indonesia, communicating God's love to children there.

The Stephensons leap to mind. Larry and Beth had always been alert in their home church to take care of our community's needy ones, the hidden people that comfortable and preoccupied Americans are usually too busy to see. But the Stephensons saw—and cared. Now they are in Somalia, feeding and binding the wounds of refugees and helping them grow crops so they can feed themselves. Love is reaching out.

Their examples—and there are hundreds more I could mention—make me examine myself. For whom am I crying? Whose wounds am I binding? Is my love reaching out? Are my hands and my mouth communicating the love of the Lord? Dr. James Stewart, when he was professor of New Testament at Edinburgh, described the greatest threat to the church in unexpected terms. He didn't point to communism or atheism or any other ism but to the attempt many Christians are making to sneak into Heaven incognito, without letting other people know they are Christians, not sharing their faith.

I can't help wondering whether they're going to make it. They claim to have faith, but they don't have love; and "anyone who does not love his brother, whom he has seen, cannot love God, whom he has not seen. And he has given us this command: Whoever loves God must also love his brother" (1 John 4:20, 21). Love never goes it alone. The Lord of Love does not pray only for himself or even only for His close friends ("My prayer is not for them alone"), but for people He hasn't even met yet ("I pray also for those who will believe in me through their message"). He takes for granted that those who love Him will reach out. (See John 17:20.)

I have been meditating on what these words mean for my own ministry. Last week I listened as our mayor outlined the growth of our city. When we moved to Arizona in 1979, Mesa had a population of 160,000 and was even then one of the fastest growing cities in America. It has kept growing. By 1984 the number had risen to 201,000, and by 2000 a projected 400,000 will be within the city limits (and another 500,000 in the surrounding East Valley area.)

Nearly a million people—and all of them need the love of the Lord.

It's my job to see that they learn about it. And receive it. The Lord of Love planted our church in this community at this time so that we can be a society of organized love that reaches out to as many people as the Lord gives us strength to serve. We know, because His Word teaches us, that the church of Jesus Christ cannot ever become self-satisfied or self-serving. The church exists primarily for the sake of those who don't yet belong to it.

So our love must reach out—and hang on!

Love Hangs On

"I pray . . . that all of them may be one, Father, just as you are in me and I am in you" (John 17:21). Unity and evangelism go together. The world won't believe in Jesus if His disciples can't get along with one another. (See John 17:21, 23.)

It's unity that He is after, not uniformity. He does not expect His disciples to sacrifice their distinctive personalities. His body is vibrant with variety. There are varieties of gifts, but there is one unifying Spirit (1 Corinthians 12).

How is unity achieved? We obviously have had trouble answering the question. When Frank Mead's *Handbook of Denominations* was published in the early 1950s, Mead counted around 260 denominations in the United States. When J. Gordon Melton's

Encyclopedia of American Religions came out in 1978, we learned that the figure had jumped to nearly 1200. In the early days of the church, people said, "Behold, how those Christians love one another." It wasn't long until their observation had to change to, "Behold, how those Christians hate one another."

Every country of our so-called enlightened Western Civilization offers its examples of religious intolerance. Since our immediate roots are in England, we are quite familiar with its infamous and often bloody battles to establish the supremacy of this or that branch of Christendom. When King Henry VIII broke with Rome and declared the Church of England independent of the Papacy, he ignited the fires of intolerance that threatened more than once to destroy the national government. When the Catholic Queen Mary succeeded to his throne, she began to kill off the country's Protestants. Elizabeth followed her and slaughtered the Catholics. Then the Stuarts claimed the throne and presided over a period of bloody confusion. When the Puritans came to power under Oliver Cromwell, they turned against the Anglicans and Catholics alike. For well over a century, gallows, whips, and prisons were employed as evangelistic tools, with the dominant religious party seldom hesitating to torture people of a contrary opinion. Each denomination was fighting for the right to be the single representative of the Prince of Peace on earth!

I wish I could say that spirit is dead. Just when I might have thought so, I read of a Baptist Church split in Bristol, Pennsylvania, which became so bitter that the dissidents hired armed guards to protect them while they held a separate service in the basement of the church. They also sued the minister for "un-Christian conduct." Seems he called a church member an old battle-ax. The church voted to fire him, but he refused to go and instead threatened to remove bodily the people who voted against him. Behold, how those Christians fight one another!

Such anti-Christian behavior has long been the object of scorn. Jonathan Swift turned his satirical powers against such wrangling in his *Gulliver's Travels,* graphically describing the Lilliputians' division over the appropriate way to crack an egg—the Big Enders versus the Little Enders. In more recent times, Dr. Seuss, the incomparable author of children's stories, published his forty-second story for youngsters, *The Butter Battle Book.* He has the arms race in mind as he chronicles the competition between the Yooks and the Zooks, who are suspicious of each other because

115

the Yooks eat their bread with the butter facing up and the Zooks prefer the butter facing down. Neither side will give, so they build more and better war machines until each side boasts its own Bitsy Big-Boy Boomeros, "filled with mysterious Moo-Lacka-Moo," which can blow the other side to Sala-ma-goo.

Seuss's book reads like a child's version of church history!

Is unity possible among Christians? It is, but only on Jesus' terms. It is evident from His prayer that Christian unity results from the merger of two essential virtues, genuine love *and* a motivating sense of mission.

I've seen how this works in one local church. One Sunday morning when one of our elders was presiding at the Communion service, he asked the members of the congregation who had come from some other fellowship to raise their hands. It looked as if at least three-fourths did so. I recognized many of them: former Methodists, Presbyterians, Baptists, Mormons, Episcopalians, Jehovah's Witnesses, and of course, many former unbelievers. All of us were about to express our unity by partaking of the Lord's Supper.

Our elder could have asked other questions, and found that we were just as diverse politically, educationally, culturally, economically, and socially as we were in religious background. We are not at all uniform, but we are united.

Our unity has two bases. The first is our common faith in Jesus as the Christ, the Son of the Living God. He is our Lord and our Savior. We obey no other master. We are in Him just as surely as He is in the Father (John 17:21, 23, 24, 26). He reached out and saved us, and He still hangs on to us.

The second basis of our unity is our shared mission. We are more than believers—we are missionaries, every one of us. As the Father sent Christ, so He has sent and is sending all His disciples to communicate His love "so that the world may believe that you have sent me" (John 17:21). We work at our unity, we make every effort to get along with one another, because Christ prayed, "May they be brought to complete unity to let the world know that you sent me and have loved them even as you have loved me" (John 17:23).

We are under orders to do everything possible to make disciples for the Lord. A fighting, disagreeable church turns the world away from the Lord.

The first time I visited the Church of the Holy Sepulchre in

116

Jerusalem, I realized as never before why Jesus so earnestly prayed—and how completely His followers have betrayed Him. The symbol of this betrayal is Holy Sepulchre. The building is in a shocking state of repair, a condition that has prevailed for decades. It probably won't ever be totally refurbished, because its proprietors can't agree even on something as simple as building reconditioning.

The Church of the Holy Sepulchre "belongs" to five denominations: Greek Orthodox, Roman Catholic, Armenian, Jacobite Syrian, and Coptic. They hold services in the building and forbid any other body to join their ranks. Hostility runs deep among them and occasionally erupts in violence. There was even the time when a riot broke out and two men were killed because a Greek had swept one more step of an outer stairway than it was his right to do. During the days of Britain's rule of Jerusalem, Moslem soldiers had to be on duty to keep the Christians from killing one another.

The Moslems weren't guiltless, either. Once an Armenian Christian brought a Jewish lady to the church. Moslems and Christians alike set on them and beat the man.

How is it possible that the disciples of the Lord of Love could turn on each other in such hatred? It is because they have forgotten their mission.

I am writing these pages in the midst of the World Series. All season, the sports pages have run stories of the wild antics of the individual players that make up these two teams. Yank the men off their teams, plunk them down with their families to live side by side in the same neighborhood, and you'll find that after a short while, most of them won't have anything to do with the rest of them. They aren't personal friends; some of them secretly despise their teammates. Yet this week you'd never know it. They are pulling together in perfect harmony, doing everything possible to help their team win the series. Championship teams learn how to create unity. They have a mission to complete, and they won't let any individual differences derail them from that mission.

That's true in all group sports, isn't it? And in music (think of the distasteful dissonance a symphony orchestra perpetrates before the conductor calls them to order and leads them to harmony. They have a mission to perform.)

It's no secret that nothing unites a nation like rising to protect the country from invasion. Unity is the by-product of mission.

So the church. We are under orders. Our Lord has commissioned us to reach out in love to serve and win the world for Him. Here He prays that we will hang on to each other so that we can effectively evangelize. Our mission is evangelism. Our motive is love. Love reaches out and takes hold of others for Christ. Love hangs on to those it holds, so that they in turn can reach out in love. So it goes until the whole world is included in the embrace of God's love.

13

WHAT DOES GOD WANT ME TO DO WITH MY LIFE?

John 21:15-19

On the campus of our nearby state university, this small advertising card was being distributed to students:

BEULAH

Reader & Advisor
I will read for you and tell you all you want to know about your past, present or future. I will give advice that will help you with your marriage, job, sweetheart or business. If you are sick, suffering, have bad luck or evil influences—see me today. Is your husband or wife faithful or not?
   If you need help, want help or just confused and don't know where to go, call me now.

2026 APACHE BLVD.
TEMPE, AZ 85281
[Phone number]

She's a good businesswoman, this Beulah. She knows her market and how to appeal to people's deepest fears. Since she has targeted college-aged young people, I can only conclude that apparently things haven't changed much on campus since the days when I was a professor. We talked a lot then about the identity crisis. Students were obsessed with such questions as, "Who am I?" and (among Christians), "What does God want me to do with my life?"

These are questions that haunt many people throughout their lives, a fact that is not lost on the likes of Beulah. She's in the business of providing quick, easy answers for hard, demanding questions. She passes herself off as a "seer," with powers to read the cards or the stars or some other signs of fate. For a reasonable monetary consideration, she can solve all your problems. In an uncertain universe, she is able to grant you certainty.

Not long ago, I had a stimulating conversation with one of our church's college students. She must have found me disturbingly vague as I wrestled with some of her genuine questions (unlike Beulah, I don't have supernatural powers, don't even own a crystal ball. For that matter, I don't even have a respectable deck of cards.) More than anything else, this young woman, a committed Christian, wanted to know what God would have her to do with her life. She needed to find herself. She felt she was drifting without any specific goals or plans for her future. What should she do?

I admired her honesty and had few pat answers for her. I did suggest, though, that the Bible offers some helpful guidelines. Several of them we have explored in this book. With the Lord of Love as our teacher and example, I told her as I have been telling you, we can't go wrong. Here's what we know for certain:

1) The Lord loves us as we are. We don't have to be afraid to give ourselves to Him.

2) We can trust Him completely. If we obey Him, we will have life.

3) If we really love Him, we'll give our all for Him.

4) We give our all for Him in humble ways, like washing dirty feet, by serving rather than by being served.

5) We don't have to be afraid of tomorrow, then, since we can serve Him in high places and low places, in prison or out of it, in life or in death.

6) We'll can keep on reaching out, loving others, and hanging on to them no matter what.

All this and much more we have learned in this study of love in the Gospel of John, and all this and more I shared with my young friend in our talk.

That conversation is still on my mind as I begin writing this final chapter, because in reading John 21:15-19, I have found just the answer I should have given her. The brief dialogue between the risen Lord and His unreliable disciple Peter summarizes everything the Gospel of John has to teach about the meaning of love. It also contains Jesus' definitive word on what God wants us to do with our lives.

To appreciate fully what is happening between Jesus and Peter, we have to go back to the beginning of their relationship and briefly trace the ups and downs of the disciple's career.

The Call

We don't know what preceded Jesus' invitation to Peter and his brother, but we can take it for granted that the fishermen had some prior acquaintance with Him. They may have been followers of John the Baptist (we know Andrew was—John 1:35-42), who had been announcing that the Messiah was coming and had then pointed to Jesus as the One. They may even have been with Jesus on earlier occasions. If so, they had already felt something of His dynamic leadership and tasted of His incredible teaching. They had never met such a person before.

Whatever the case, Matthew 4:18, 19 narrates the event of Peter's call in these simple words: "As Jesus was walking beside the Sea of Galilee, he saw two brothers, Simon called Peter and his brother Andrew. They were casting a net into the lake, for they were fishermen. 'Come, follow me,' Jesus said, 'and I will make you fishers of men.' At once they left their nets and followed him."

Just like that. They hand over their fishing business to someone else, bid farewell to their families, and attach themselves to Jesus. These fishers of fish accept the promotion: they will become fishers of men. They will let Jesus use what they already are to develop them into what God wants them to become.

That is the first step in doing what God wants you to do with your life. You obey His invitation to follow Jesus.

Apprenticeship

Then you become His disciple—that is, His apprentice. Like Peter and Andrew, you learn everything that you can about and from Jesus.

Here it would be helpful to stop reading this book and pick up the Gospel of Mark for a quick review the life of the apprentice Simon Peter. Most scholars believe that this Gospel is based on Peter's reminiscences about Jesus, because there is so much about him in it. Here we see him at his best and at his worst.

Mark presents Peter listening intently to his Master's voice, struggling to fit the new knowledge into his traditional training; observing his Master's healing powers and trying to imitate them; experimenting on his own when Jesus sends the disciples out two by two to widen the scope of the Lord's ministry; and growing ever so slowly into the leader Jesus is convinced he can become. Jesus has started with good material, however, since Peter is what

121

we have learned today to call a strong natural leader, always out in front, quick to speak, eager to be taught, and the first to risk making a mistake.

Becoming an apprentice of Jesus, like Peter and his brother Andrew, then, is our second step in doing what God wants us to do with our lives. It is one thing to answer the Lord's call to follow Him; it is quite another and more difficult—but equally essential—thing actually to follow!

We twentieth-century apprentices, as eager as Peter to grow into good disciples, cannot then be content with just studying the words of the Master; we have to be doers of His word as well as readers. We must follow Him. A disciple is not merely a student of Jesus—he is an apprentice who learns by doing.

Crisis

The third step is to submit to the test of loyalty to the Lord—and pass it.

Peter failed his.

His crisis came in the final days of Jesus' ministry. For many weeks, the Lord had been predicting His death in Jerusalem, but no one would really believe Him. They had such confidence in Him that they couldn't—they wouldn't—imagine that any force on earth could defeat Him. They hadn't yet caught on to the fact that God's ways are not always the world's ways, and that He sometimes uses what looks like a defeat to achieve total victory.

The last time Jesus makes this prediction is at the table on that fateful night of what we now call the Last Supper. (See Mark 14.) He has just startled His friends by announcing that one of them is a traitor. Then, adding insult to injury, He predicts that every one of them will fall away.

That's too much for Peter. "Even if all fall away, I will not," he protests (Mark 14:29). He means it, too. He has already sacrificed everything for Jesus over their years together. What is there to lose that he hasn't already given up?

Jesus doesn't dispute Peter's sincerity, but neither does He waver from His prophecy. "I tell you the truth, today—yes, tonight—before the rooster crows twice you yourself will disown me three times" (Mark 14:30).

Peter can't stand it. "Even if I have to die with you," he explodes, "I will never disown you." The other disciples echo his sentiments (Mark 14:31).

122

There isn't a deliberate liar in the group. They speak honestly, but they speak naively. They are a virtuous group, but theirs is an untried virtue. They haven't faced a real crisis yet. It's coming, though. When it comes, Peter crumbles. While Jesus suffers His mock trial before the Jewish Supreme Court (the Sanhedrin), Peter goes on the defense in his own mini-trial out in the courtyard. His prosecuting attorney is a young servant girl. She spots that he is a stranger in their midst; this is Judea, and Peter is a Galilean, like Jesus. "You also were with that Nazarene, Jesus," she accuses him.

"I don't know or understand what you're talking about," he snaps at her and huffs off. But she sees him a little later and repeats the charge, this time to those around her. "This fellow is one of them." Again he denies it.

The seed of suspicion has been planted and before long others standing around take up the servant girl's case: "Surely you are one of them, for you are a Galilean." With curses befitting a journeyman fisherman, Peter closes his defense. "I don't know this man you're talking about."

And the rooster crows the second time. Peter breaks down and cries. (See Mark 14:66-72.)

The third step in knowing the will of God for our lives then is this: putting our discipleship to the test.

But what will happen to us if we, like Peter, fail?

Reassurance

This fourth step is not something we can do. When we have denied the Lord or betrayed His trust in us, we have no right to expect anything from Him. We have rejected Him; the relationship is over. What hold can we possibly have on someone we have publicly denounced?

The Lord of Love has to make the next move. This He does on the morning of His resurrection. The scene is recorded in Mark 16:1-8. When Mary Magdalene, Mary the mother of James, and Salome go to Jesus' tomb to anoint His body with burial oil and spices, they are amazed to find Jesus gone and an angel standing before them.

Peter must have been equally amazed when they reported what the angel told them. "Go, tell his disciples *and Peter*. . . ." He was the only disciple singled out by name. He was as guilty as Judas, yet the Lord made certain that Peter receive these words of

123

reassurance. He's still in the group. The Lord of Love wants him!

This fourth step is essential for every sinner among us to understand. I have already said that we can't take the step, but the Lord must. I was only half right. The initiative does depend on Him, but the step is not completed until we act. We must accept our acceptance. Now we are ready for the final step.

Renewal

"Peter, do you truly love me?"

They have just finished eating breakfast from the enormous catch Jesus has helped them bring in from the Sea of Galilee. When Peter and his fellow fishermen spotted Jesus on the shore, they didn't recognize Him at first. He was just a helpful fellow who shouted to them to throw their nets on the other side of their boat. They'd had an unsuccessful night, but they heeded the stranger's advice and brought up a huge catch. Then one of the disciples realized that the stranger was Jesus.

With his customary impulsiveness, Peter jumps into the water, leaving his buddies to finish the work (it is characteristic of impulsive people to leave the labor to others). My guess is that Peter is so grateful to be back in the Jesus' good graces he wants never to leave the Master's side from then on. He has so much making up to do.

It's a normal urge, isn't it? When we've done wrong, even though we've been forgiven, we want to make up for the damage we've done. Jesus gives Peter that chance now. That's what His questions are all about. He is giving Peter the opportunity to renew himself.

"Simon, son of John, do you truly love me more than these?" Three times He asks the questions, varying them just slightly (John 21:15, 16, 17). What exactly does He mean? There are three possible interpretations.

1) "Do you love me more than these fish and all the rest of the trappings of your trade? You left them once to follow me. Will you do it again, even though you have experienced what you'll have to suffer to be my disciple?" It is a question the Lord has to ask all of us, isn't it? Just how willing are we to give up business, income, security, and comfort for the Lord?

2) "Do you love me more than you love these friends of yours? Are you now able to stick with me even if others don't approve of

what you are doing? Does what I think of you matter more than their opinion of you?" We so easily conform to this world's expectations of us, because we depend more than we like to admit on the the positive judgments of our peers. We want to be liked, so we conform. Do we have the strength to be Jesus' friends, even if we are the only ones He has?

3) "Do you love me more than you think these friends love me? You once said you did. You said that even if every one of them would deny me, you wouldn't. You've always been at the head of the line, the leader of the pack. Is that really love, or just impulsiveness? Are you willing now, as you weren't earlier, to stick with me even if nobody else does?"

Each time Jesus asks, Peter insists that the Lord knows Peter loves Him. (We would have to ask, however, how Peter can expect the Lord to count on him, since Peter hasn't proved trustworthy so far.) Words aren't enough anymore. Peter has used words before and Jesus found out that's all they were, just words. Now He demands action.

Here, Peter, is how you can prove you love me. "Take care of my sheep" (John 21:16).

We should have anticipated Jesus' command. Here, at the end of the Gospel that teaches us so much about the Lord of Love, Jesus is as consistent as ever. He doesn't give Peter something "religious" to do to renew his life. No acts of penance, no specified good deeds that will enable him to work his way back into the Lord's favor, no special prayers or rituals to perform. Instead, the Good Shepherd asks His apprentice to imitate his Master. He is now to become a shepherd, taking care of others who need the ministrations of the Lord of Love. It's steady work, undazzling, undramatic, often unrewarding. A shepherd's days are marked by duty, often more like drudgery rather than exhilaration. But if the shepherd is faithful, the lives of the sheep are saved. "Simon, feed my lambs."

Jesus renews Peter by giving him a job to do.

Remember my young college friend, trying so desperately to find herself? How would Jesus deal with her? The same way He helps another sinner find his way. Jesus would have her go to work taking care of His sheep.

My friend's problem is that she is so distraught over what the Lord wants her to do with her life in the future that she is withholding herself from Him in the present. She looks at her college years as preparation for the service she'll give the Lord *someday*. In the meantime, she isn't serving. She feels as lost as Peter did before the Lord reassured him and renewed his life by making him an instrument of God's love on earth.

What she is learning is what most of us have already learned: we don't know who we are apart from our job. Our self-identity is all tied up with our work. When we men first meet each other, our first question is usually, "What do you do?" When our daughters bring their dates home to meet their parents, they can count on their father's asking at least this one: "What do you do?" If I get to ask another questions, it almost invariably is, "What does your dad do?" It's the way we men identify each other.

It's not a peculiarly male trait, either. Women find their identity in the same way. They are wives or mothers or career women—or wives or mothers *and* career women. In a mobile society like ours, where we meet each other first as strangers and not as long-time fellow townspeople who have known each others' families for generations, we identify ourselves by our jobs.

Jesus renews Peter's life by giving him the biggest job in the world. He builds on Peter's original call: you are to become a fisher of men, He said in the beginning. You are to catch men. (Remember—love reaches out.) Now I want you also to take care of them, like a shepherd. (Love hangs on.)

Jesus gives Peter new eyesight. When he denied Christ, Peter was looking after Peter's welfare and no one else's. Jesus was going down to defeat. Peter had to save himself, even if everyone else should be lost.

Now Jesus calls him to see the needs of others—more than see, *do* something for others. When you look at the world through Jesus' eyes, you can't waste much time feeling sorry for yourself. The Lord of Love sees sheep without a shepherd, sick people without a physician, hungry people without food. You can never be calloused about others when you love them, and you can never be content looking after your own interests. "Peter, feed my lambs."

A man was visiting the English coast in Cornwall. While he was admiring the powerful beauty of the waves crashing against the rocks below him, a boy from the area walked toward him. The visitor commented on the majesty of the scene, but the boy was unimpressed. "If your people were fishermen," he told him, "you wouldn't say that. Our boats are out today."

126

People he loved were in danger. He couldn't forget them. What a stranger can passively enjoy, a lover becomes passionately involved with. He sees through the eyes of love.

It is instructive, isn't it, that the job Jesus gave Peter was that of a humble servant. I think of that every time the Vatican elects a new pope. Cardinals assemble from all over the world to place a gleaming crown on the man they insist is the descendant of Peter. They crown him and place a scepter in his hands; they kneel before him and kiss his ring. He rules the church.

Jesus, having taught Peter to see the sheep without a shepherd, doesn't give him a crown, but an assignment. He is to serve the sheep, not be served by them. He is to humble himself. He is to love as his Master loved. He is to forget himself in his service for others. His is the labor; God's is the glory.

We have come to the end of our study and find ourselves at the beginning. In the first chapter, we learned that Jesus is like His Father, coming to save His own for no other reason than God is like that. He loves us and will do whatever is necessary to rescue us.

In this last chapter is the proof that the Son is like the Father. From beginning to end, His love has remained constant, as His relationship with Peter demonstrates. He loved Peter in the beginning enough to call him into His circle of intimate friends. Even after Peter deserted Him, His love never wavered. He restored His disciple to favor and renewed his call, this one building on the first. "Follow me and I will make you a fisher of men," He charged him in the beginning. In the end, however, the fisherman is to become a shepherd like his Master. "Take care of my sheep." A fisher of men reaches out in love; a shepherd of souls hangs on with a love that will not let go.

That's because a disciple of Christ reaches out in love and hangs on.

That's because Jesus reaches out and hangs on.

Like Father like Son.

LEROY LAWSON
SHARES THE SECRET

The secret of living an extraordinary life. In *The Lord of Promises,* you will learn how to claim thirteen of Jesus' most powerful promises as your own! Order #39989 (Instructor, #39988).

The secrets of the kingdom of Heaven. Jesus told His disciples they could know what the ancient sages longed to know—and He revealed those secrets in parables. In *The Lord of Parables,* Lawson shows you how you can know them, too. Order #39981 (Instructor, #39980).

The secret of church growth. *Introducing Church Growth* and *Church Growth: Everybody's Business,* by Lawson and Tetsunano Yamamori, contain practical principles to help churches of any size to grow. Order #40002 and #40035.